Beyond the CV

Securing a Lifetime of Work in the Global Market

Helen Vandevelde

Butterworth-Heinemann
Linacre House, Jordan Hill, Oxford OX2 8DP
A division of Reed Educational and Professional Publishing Ltd

A member of the Reed Elsevier plc group

OXFORD   BOSTON   JOHANNESBURG
MELBOURNE   NEW DEHLI   SINGAPORE
FIRST PUBLISHED 1997

British Library Cataloguing in Publication Data
A catalogue record for this book is available from the British
Library

ISBN 0 7506 3653 X

Typeset by Florencetype Ltd, Stoodleigh, Devon
Printed and bound in Great Britain by
Biddles Ltd, Guildford and King's Lynn

Contents

Preface   *vii*

Introduction   *x*

1. The New Work Order   *1*

2. The Impact of Technology   *29*

3. Attitudes to Work   *52*

4. Creating Opportunity from the Global Market   *78*

5. Cerebral Fibres: Making Good the Education Deficit   *110*

6. The Global Nomad   *141*

7. The Digital Portfolio: Career Strategies beyond the Lifetime Career   *194*

8. Conclusion: And beyond the Portfolio . . .?   *220*

References and Further Reading   *225*

Useful websites   *227*

Index   *229*

Preface

There's so much pessimism around about the future of work that this book was crying out to be written. The anxiety and despair I have witnessed in discussions with people, especially under the age of thirty, have had the intensity of shards still warm from the explosion.

And yet a carnival of opportunity is being created by the global economy, just waiting to be exploited by those with a fair degree of imagination, combined with determination and self-belief. In countless seminars and individual discussions, most of all with young people on the threshold of their careers, I've found so much pent-up energy and inspiration eager for tangible evidence that the groundwork they're engaged in will turn out to have been a sound and worthwhile investment.

Such self-investment in expertise, skills, attitudes and personal qualities is both essential and beneficial, of course, if its direction is tuned in to the nature of the marketplace in which those assets will be traded. In addition to providing evidence of the expanding nature of the opportunities being generated by the global market, this book also aims to enable you to articulate your career strategy to wider ambitions and horizons and to prepare yourself for potentially new challenges on an informed and pragmatic basis.

Thus another feature of this book is its promotion of reflection and planning through a series of practical activities. Accordingly, it has not been written as an academic treatise. It has a research base, of course; and the more significant sources are listed at the end of the book. I have not made specific references to news material that has been reported in the press and the personnel and management literature.

Where I have differed from the prevailing trend in the more serious literature on the nature of the career and the future of work is in declining to add to the cottage industry which has developed over the last couple of decades, built around down-beat predictions which, however elegantly argued, leave the aspiring careerist in an entrail-laden tumbrel of despair.

We have to take the world of employment as it is (or as this book argues, as it will be in years to come), and devise strategies for achievement and fulfilment. As you would expect with a book which stresses the importance of individual action, you will find an upbeat — but not rose-tinted — approach to the challenge of mapping out realistic courses of action for the increasingly volatile economic and organizational conditions we shall all have to negotiate.

My research for this book has brought me into contact with expert witnesses who without exception were fired with enthusiasm about careers futures and optimism for those who were prepared to work hard on their career strategies and their self-investment. I am grateful to them for their contributions and hope I have been able to convey a flavour of their inspirational confidence in what the coming century has in store for new and recent entrants to the global labour market.

My thanks go to Yvonne Baker, international sales manager; Dr Christopher Bissell, head of department of telematics at the Open University; Jonathan Bratt, global account director at A. C. Nielsen; Professor Chris Brewster, director of the Centre for European Human Resource Management at Cranfield University; Terry Caine, Euroadviser with the Overseas Placing Unit; Mick Carey, director of Careers Europe; Debra Hawkins, European sales manager; Stephanie James, policy executive at the British Chambers of Commerce; Jane Kingsley, managing director with Russell Reynolds Associates, the recruitment consultancy; Denise Lincoln, human resources director of Allied Domecq; Eryl McNally, Member of the European Parliament for Milton Keynes and Bedfordshire; Philip Morgan, sales manager with a multinational company; Mark Richards, portfolio worker; Dr Jonathan Stock, lecturer in music at Durham University; David Taylor, employment development manager at Anglian Water; Colm Tobin, careers consultant at University College Dublin; George Turnbull, director of public relations at the Associated Examining Board; Rachel Tyson, portfolio worker; Tony Webb, director of education at the Confederation of British Industry; Dr Dick Whitcutt, director, Industry in Education; and Graham Whitehead, advanced concepts manager at British Telecommunications.

I also interviewed a number of mature students at the INSEAD European school of business administration at Fontainebleau and at Cranfield University, as well as a group of first degree university students. One of the chapters in this book is entitled the "global nomad" and these perceptive, energetic and sensitive people are models of the explosive talents that a global career can unleash as well as demand.

My thanks, then, to Louis-Dominique Bouzy, Jacquie Brighouse, Bridget Jackson, Ruth Knight, Monique Manton, Diego Massidda, Rory McMahon, Per Pundsnes, Alex Rink, Richard Steele, Susan Welford, Abbi Wilson and Susanna Wong. Helle Jensen proved a model of patience and resourcefulness as public relations officer at INSEAD. I am also grateful to Jacquie Shanahan and Diane Scarlett at Butterworth-Heinemann for their helpful suggestions and constant encouragement.

One of the unintended outcomes of the work I completed at the research stage for this book was the more or less even gender balance which emerged as I drew up my shortlist of expert witnesses and informants. Perhaps this might be a modest indication that the global market will turn out to be a generator of opportunities which is gender neutral. On the other hand English is not a gender neutral language. Let me explain here that one convention I have followed in my use of pronouns is the random use of masculines and feminines.

Finally my family insisted that I record their gratitude for the fact that I kept out of their way for the whole period that I was writing this book. Their constant and uninhibited encouragement to me to write another book has been touching . . .

Helen Vandevelde
helenvandevelde@dial.pipex.com

Introduction

You might suspect there's something pretty audacious about a book called *Beyond the CV*. After all, when you browse the careers shelves of bookshops, you could think you'd mistakenly stumbled into the pulp fiction or natural history (shark-infested waters) galleries, given the number of books that tell you how to write a killer CV or to pursue a razor-sharp career. Going by the number of titles available with the letters "CV" in them, they look pretty much alive and kicking.

I would answer the suspicion by saying you were right: this is an ambitious book. It rejects the orthodox approach of stringing together optimistic strands of advice about how to organize your career, devoid of context and evidence about how the work environment will change in future.

Instead, it appeals to those enterprising spirits who want to map out their careers intelligently, on the basis of empirical evidence about the economic, technological and organizational factors that over the next five or ten years will make the whole concept of career very different from what it is now.

This is, then, a book for the future. It explores what careers will become. Not what they are now.

It's also a book that looks outwards from the UK to the global environment. It examines how the global economy is changing the nature of work contracts, and what we need to do now to be ahead of organizational requirements as they mutate.

Most important of all, it assesses the implications of developments in the global economy and in information and communication technology and, by anticipating how these forces will impact upon the world of work, generates a network of activities designed to prepare you for the concept that the word "career" will represent beyond the turn of the century.

It's a challenging book also because it invites you to think hard about your future too, through a series of activities which will help you to shape your career through the uncertainties of change. So if you want handed to you on a plate a career plan that sees you through the pulsating and often bewildering maelstrom of business endeavour, you might as well be looking on the pulp fiction shelves.

What I'm suggesting is:

- if you don't do the thinking behind your career plan yourself, it won't be of any value to you
- it's no good just keeping up with the times — you have to get ahead of them
- if you have an understanding of the dynamics behind changes in the organization of work, you will be best placed to deal with them effectively within your career
- if you have a career horizon that looks out beyond the UK, you will develop a lateral approach to career planning which opens up opportunities even as the competition for work intensifies.

In your bid to secure your future in the twenty-first century global market you can turn an experience akin to surfing on a sea of sulphuric acid into an exhilarating enterprise which offers personal fulfilment in addition to career success. This book encourages you to assess and develop your skills, attitudes and behaviours in the light of developments which will be considered a normal part of life in five to ten years' time, but many of which are only just beginning to enter the public consciousness.

These developments include:

- demographic changes in work participation
- the impact of computer-based technologies on the organization of work
- the tantalizing potential of communications technology to generate new organizational forms
- the emergence of ambivalent attitudes to work
- the diversification of work contracts
- the global economy
- the fragmentation of political power
- the spread of globally consistent recruitment practices
- the growth of virtual companies
- the primacy of human resources for the generation of wealth
- the pervasiveness of multicultural and multinational team working
- the increasing willingness among employees to be assertive with their employers over their attitudes to career investment
- the "dematerialization" of the sources of wealth creation
- the dynamic giving rise to the "global nomad".

These forces need to be factored into the calculations we make about our individual careers. They are so powerful that we can no longer afford to compile CVs which are the autobiographical equivalent of stamp collections: moribund compendiums of passive archives.

On the contrary, we need to anticipate the changes that will occur in the years ahead and both to develop the talents we need to thrive in their midst and to create the opportunities to demonstrate them in a format that brings them to life.

The portfolio you devise will be an animated representation of your abilities, bringing to life on screen your unique blend of skills, expertise, attitudes and personality traits. The digital portfolio which is set to replace the orthodox CV will claw at the attention of the awarders of work contracts, because you will have crafted the experience it encapsulates through negotiation with employers and others whom you have persuaded to support you in your endeavour.

Welcome to the challenge of the global market and to the prospect of security, beyond the CV.

The New Work Order

We are on the threshold of the age of the female breadwinner. The 1997 British labour force projections indicate that women will make up over 45 per cent of the workforce by 2006. This prediction coincides with the most intense period of national self-doubt about the future of work since the Great Depression of the 1920s and 1930s.

Changes in the nature of employment are having a widespread impact on the composition of the labour force. Women and the self-employed have increased their share of employment in the 1990s and this trend will continue into the next century. The proportion of people over the age of thirty-five within the labour market will continue to grow. The thirty-five to forty-four year old age group will make up the largest proportion of the workforce in 2006.

Such demographic and social trends affecting the new work order need to be factored into individual career strategies designed for the challenges of the global labour market. Understanding and anticipating changes in the demand for labour and in patterns of career opportunities are essential to planning a strategy for survival and prosperity in the global economy.

The life of Kylie

Increasing numbers of family units in the UK have experienced the emergence of the female as the main or sole source of income. Most working women in western Europe too now contribute more than half of their family's income. Both male and female employment have undergone structural changes in recent decades.

There have been significant changes in the types of employment that men have in the labour market. In the past twenty-five years the proportion of men working in manufacturing has fallen

1

from 41 per cent to 28 per cent. More than 85 per cent of men born in the 1940s had full-time jobs when they were thirty years old. The figure for thirty year olds born in the 1960s has fallen to below 70 per cent. During the past ten years the number of men working part-time has increased by more than 40 per cent. The number of male temporary workers has also been increasing.

Changes in the country's industrial structure have resulted in the creation of jobs that are more attractive to women. In 1950 women made up just one-third of the labour force. By 1992 43 per cent of women were in work. Economic activity rates for women aged twenty and over are projected to increase, the biggest gains indicated for the twenty-five to thirty-four year old cohort in the years up to 2006. Women have secured two-thirds of the fifteen million new jobs created in the European Union between 1980 and 1992. Women are expected to make up three-quarters of the 1.2 million additional people expected to be in work in the UK by 2006.

During the 1980s, the number of self-employed people increased by one million. Admittedly this growth was concentrated in construction and the service sector. The collapse of the construction industry in the early 1990s reined back this growth. But research by Business Strategies in 1996 suggests that self-employment will rise to 13.4 per cent of total employment by 2001.

There is a stratification in self-employment as there is in the rest of the labour market. At the bottom end, there are people working for themselves in conditions as dispiriting as the sweat-shops of the nineteenth century, with sewing the most prominent activity, followed by packing, clerical work, routine assembly and knitting.

At the other extreme there is tremendous buoyancy in niches characterized by specialist expertise and in consultancy. Although men still make up three-quarters of the self-employed, that proportion is projected to decline as an increasing number of women opt for more independent economic activity.

Change breeds opportunity. Targeted thinking for the global market requires us to overcome the pessimism of the moment, to assess the opportunities generated by change and then to make career investment plans on the basis of that assessment.

Thinking for the global market

When the Institute of Management asked 1000 UK managers what their worries were about the future, over half highlighted what they saw as dwindling job opportunities for their children. Nearly half were also fearful of their own chances of remaining in work from middle age onwards. Misgivings about their ability to hold onto their current jobs came close behind.

Although the prognosis for employment conditions in the long term is not uniformly pessimistic for all age groups, the most cursory glance at the newspapers reveals a growing expectation of adversity to come. Millennial hacks equate the career-minded executive to a cat walking on hot porcupine quills. Even the good news, such as the projections about the increased employment of women, comes tinged with the expectation that the majority of new jobs taken up by women will be part-time, temporary and low paid.

But there are opportunities for vibrant economic activity in any changing situation. The shifting age profile in the UK and the rest of the European Union provides an alluring example. The increase in adult life expectancy will cause the number of people over the age of sixty to double by the year 2025. By that date there will be 140 million over-sixties in the European Union, many with disposable wealth accumulated through pensions, investments and inheritance. They will then make up nearly one-third of the total population. Their consumption of health services, welfare support, leisure and other services will create a huge demand that will need to be met by the working population.

No nation in Europe will escape from the impact of this development. The UK's elderly will increase by 44 per cent by 2025. At the same time the working population of the UK will decline by 2.8 per cent. In other European countries, the prospects are starker, with Germany, for example, experiencing a 51 per cent increase in its over-sixties and a 13.5 per cent fall in its working-age population.

Thus at the same time as the European Union's working population falls, especially outside the UK, the European Union will also need an increase in economic activity to support its growing numbers of old people. Although this will exert tremendous pressure on European welfare systems, it will also place career strategists who have had the foresight to invest in their mobility, global communication and survival skills at a premium.

What is needed, for a career strategy which goes beyond the demands of the traditional CV, is an understanding of the diverse, ambiguous and often contradictory trends which govern the employment market. This understanding needs to be used as a basis for developing more flexible approaches to achieving a secure income stream over half a lifetime.

Such a strategy also demands an understanding that change is a source of opportunity. Paralysis occasioned by fear and indecision isn't an option. Five intrinsic attributes for success in the global market are:

- confidence informed by sound analysis
- decision making based on a willingness to take calculated risks
- reflection supported by breadth of experience
- generation of options infused by imagination
- commitment to self-investment animated by energy and enthusiasm.

Merchants of doom

My father had a working life of 100 000 hours. I could now produce the equivalent output in 20 000 hours. And my son will be able to generate the same amount in 1000 hours. He will do it differently, with technology to help him.

The end-of-the-world-is-nigh industry has locked onto technological advances to locate both the traditional job and the lifetime career in its sights. An intellectual indulgence previously dominated by fringe religions throughout the centuries has suddenly become fashionable in more mainstream disciplines.

Is this gnawing insecurity a media puff talked up by writers, politicians and assorted peddlers of cataclysm? When Charles Handy writes about portfolio working, or William Bridges argues in *Jobshift* that the very concept of "the career" is outdated, are they describing current developments and extrapolating them into the future as illustrations of the inevitable? Or are they merely speculating about the organizational shapes and corresponding career strategies which they believe will be successful?

Perhaps this outbreak of designer despair represents nothing more sinister than an inevitable manifestation of millennial menopause. The recent crop of *The End of . . .* titles, pronouncing upon the end of history, the end of the nation state, the end of print, the end of work as we know it, merely accords to terminal decline the status of "new chic".

Charles Handy's work has been pounced upon by those who would have us believe that dwindling numbers in the industrialized countries will enjoy secure employment into the next century. However, books like *The Age of Unreason*, *The Empty Raincoat* and *Beyond Certainty* aren't laced with the toxic cocktail of despair that many commentators have extracted from them. On the contrary, Handy proposes an alternative career strategy which many would find attractive.

Rather than have us cling desperately to the traditional job as though we were sitting on ice floes in a tropical ocean, Handy proposes a work environment in which we each move from contract to contract as portfolio workers, enhancing our employability by a combination of continuous reinvestment in our own skills and expertise, and exploitation of each contract that we complete as the springboard from which to promote ourselves to potential future employers.

That work experience, according to Handy, can be presented as part of a renewable portfolio designed to secure one contract after another, as we work not as employees, but as freelance operators willing to offer our services on a time-defined basis.

The problem with the employability debate as it has been conducted in many newspapers and journals, is that it presents two artificial alternatives neither of which is properly grounded in empirical evidence. But like the University boat race, you feel compelled to take sides, so that almost by default you become classified as a classic job-for-lifer or as an advocate of portfolio working.

The evidence is more ambiguous, as is the appropriate range of career strategies. An interesting feature of Handy's work is his use of examples to support his portfolio thesis, which are largely drawn from the ranks of the self-employed, and those whose expertise is associated with the visual and hearing senses: architects, people in advertising, musicians, designers, composers of jingles and so on.

For these professionals, the discipline of maintaining a portfolio has been *de rigueur* for half a century or more. Similarly, the self-employed – from builders to accountants – are well accustomed to using their current work in progress as a basis from which to acquire new contracts. Portfolio workers are by no means a phenomenon of the 1990s. At the same time, something fundamental is happening to the traditional career. It no longer clings limpet-like to a single organization for half a century.

Earning by midnight toil

At surface level some trends support the employment meltdown thesis. The European Commission believes that the nine-to-five job is going the way of the traditional English breakfast. Nearly half the employees in the European Union have jobs involving flexible patterns of working.

The UK leads the pack, with 66 per cent of employees working outside the traditional daylight routine. A recent European Commission study predicts an increase in flexible working patterns, especially in service industries and with the rise of teleworking.

In 1996 a consortium of researchers, *Personnel Today*, Plantime and Peterborough Software, found an increasing movement towards flexible working. They predicted that contract working would expand over the next five years. They also detected an increase in annualized hours, i.e. employment contracts that state how many hours the contract holder will work during the next twelve months. They reported that the proportion of organizations increasing contract working had more than doubled in three years.

Full-time workers now make up less than half the UK workforce. The number of people working part time has doubled since the early 1970s. Over one million people have two or more jobs at the same time. Increasing numbers are moving into and between temporary and part-time jobs.

An Institute of Management *Survey of Long-term Employment Strategies* (1995) has found that almost 90 per cent of the UK's leading employers use part-time and temporary workers. Most of these employers predict that over the next four years the use of temporary workers will increase further. Seventy per cent of them contract out part of their operations in preference to employing people directly to do the work. Again, most foresee an increase in contracting out over the next few years.

The growth of part-time and temporary jobs in the UK is taking place mainly in the service industries, such as those areas contracted out from the public sector, including catering, premises management, telecommunications and financial services.

It's also spreading to areas of manufacturing, including engineering, metals, minerals and chemicals. One example is the
Compaq manufacturing plant at Erskine, Scotland, which employs
a core workforce of 1500, but with an additional 700 on flexible
contracts.

The organization, Business Strategies, goes further, estimating
that by 2006 nearly half the workforce could be covered by flexible
arrangements such as temporary contracts, self-employment and
part-time jobs.

Contract labour

Many companies are attracted to employing people as permanent casuals – seat warmers in jobs that have a limited shelf life
because of growing automation. There is also a long-term move
away from unskilled to highly skilled work. Those with lower skill
levels are increasingly vulnerable to casual working and declining
wages.

Even in the public sector, the traditional haven of the job
for life, there are redundancies and short-term contracts. Social
workers, teachers, civil servants, even nurses, have lost their jobs
as local budget management has begun to bite.

Work has disappeared in large public sector operations which
used to operate strict demarcation lines between jobs. Employees
have become more versatile and multiskilled. Employers want
people who can move between jobs, responding to customer
demand as it fluctuates. The broader their span of knowledge
about the organization they work for, the more options are available to their managers to deploy them flexibly.

There is a long-term context in which this movement towards
job flexibility is operating. In *The Tom Peters Seminar: Crazy
Times Call for Crazy Organisations*, Peters argues that the idea
of people working for a long period in a single organization is
relatively new. It has only ever applied to a minority. The vast
majority of people have always worked in all kinds of odd jobs,
either for themselves or for small firms, in unstable settings. The
big employer providing long-term job security may turn out to
have been a historical blip.

Thus while many commentators argue that economic pressures,
advances in technology and new management techniques are
interacting to bring the whole concept of the career into question,

others are more upbeat in highlighting the opportunities arising from the growing proportion of work that no longer comes in traditional, job-sized packages. They argue that, as traditional careers give way to new work configurations which are hazy and difficult to predict, individual versatility provides a renewable source of survival and prosperity.

Dick Whitcutt, director of the organization Industry in Education, doesn't see the growing incidence of serial contracts as cause for pessimism. "I don't think people need to worry, because the right people, the people who can develop the right skills, will be mapping out the next job before they've finished the previous one. As often as not, they will be talent scouted from within the company they're already working for."

Some companies are welding the use of fixed-term employment contracts onto the concept of a career strategy. At IBM in the UK, graduates join for a fixed four-year contract. That's a significant change from the previous expectation of a lifetime career in one of the world's most successful companies. But it focuses the minds of the contract holders and gives them enough time to develop a portfolio of experience which will attract a future employer or prepare them for self-employment.

Fixed term, temporary and annualized contracts provide as many opportunities as they close off. Temporary contracts aren't as insecure as they used to be. For example, if you have a number of part-time, temporary contracts operating side by side, redundancy is not the all or nothing exercise that it is for those in a permanent, full-time job. You have greater flexibility about the hours you work: both the total number and where they are grouped during the week.

Many people are launching themselves into new part-time, temporary or self-employed careers, having taken a retirement package from their company. This has been a particular growth area in the public sector, including local government and education.

Flexible contracts can work as much to the benefit of the individual employee as to that of the company. The employee can afford to tell the company that it gets what it pays for. This is in contrast to full-time workers who often feel the obligation to work well beyond their contracted hours as part of their psychological contract.

When one compares the actual hourly rate of full-time workers, against that of (often nominally lower paid) part-time workers, the difference in remuneration between the two is not always that great. There are opportunities, then, to make flexible working operate to the advantage of the employee.

Command performance

One estimate suggests that, by 2020, less than 2 per cent of the whole global workforce will be engaged in factory work. Assembly line workers will be eliminated from the production process over the next twenty-five years. The move from mass labour to élite workforces is the distinctive feature of the information age, as compared to the industrial age.

In the late eighteenth and early nineteenth centuries, the Luddites retaliated against the machines which replicated, by tens or hundreds, manufacturing processes that had previously been done through the literal meaning of "manufacture", i.e. by hand.

A much broader spectrum of twenty-first century work output will be subject to processes that can be replicated across the globe through the use of standardized software: accounting, general practice, a host of administrative functions, training and so on.

The futile attempts of the Luddites to hold back the tide of economics by destroying the machines that cut their wages and put them out of work will strike a chord (in spirit at least) with many turn of the millennium workers whose jobs will be performed "by default", i.e. according to standard settings and global commands which feature on the software they use.

The Industrial Revolution that perplexed the Luddites was the source of a huge net increase in work. The downside was associated with the dislocation and unprecedented social conditions created as a result. Much of the current debate about the future of work emphasizes the threats unleashed by the information and communication revolution, without taking account of the opportunities which will arise for those with the foresight and flexibility to prepare appropriately.

Manufacturing a crisis?

Warwick University's Institute for Employment Research has shown how in the early 1990s the UK lost around 400 000 manufacturing jobs. It also predicts a further fall of 200 000 for the remainder of the 1990s.

One theory suggests that the trend will accelerate for manufacturing to be relocated from the industrialized countries to the
developing world, where labour costs are lower. However, the
Organization for Economic Co-operation and Development argues
that the likelihood of outflows of foreign direct investment in
manufacturing from the industrialized world has been exaggerated.

The Organization concludes that the share of low-skilled labour,
which accounted for a quarter of total production costs in the
1970s, now represents only 5–10 per cent of costs in developed
economies. As research, development and technological investment occupy an increasingly important role in the production
process, the competitive advantage of low wages is eroding.

A second reason working against an increase in foreign direct
investment in developing countries is that modern production
methods are more uncompromising in requiring quality and reliability. This reduces the attraction of manufacturing in developing
countries, because educational standards in many developing
nations are still well behind those of the developed nations. Firms
are wary of possible difficulties in finding suitably skilled workers
to apply fairly complex technologies.

Even at its most pessimistic, the manufacturing meltdown thesis
still creates opportunities for those with the attitudes and skills
to forge new opportunities from such fluctuating working conditions. However automated the manufacturing processes, products
still have to be designed, organized, priced, promoted, marketed,
sold, taxed and accounted for to shareholders.

All these functions can be effected remotely from the site of
manufacture. So even if the bulk of manufacturing were to be
exported, these tertiary functions will still be available for talented
people to perform anywhere in the world.

On active service

Erosion of the employment base in manufacturing will be offset
by the accelerating growth in the service sector, particularly in
hotels, catering, health and education, with the retail sector also
increasing employment.

However, there are fears that job creation in the service sector
might not last for much longer, as it too is subject to automation.
This sector represents over two-thirds of the total employment in

the European Union. It has been largely protected from labour-saving technical changes up until now. But as with other sectors, each segment will experience fluctuating demand for labour.

The pessimists maintain that information and communication technology will threaten vast numbers of white collar workers. These include people in banking, insurance and the wholesale and retail sectors. The managers and service providers who stay on are being converted into small, highly skilled, professional work teams, using advanced software and telecommunications technologies.

Data inputting, data processing, risk assessment, tendering, contracting and claims processing are all being put onto electronic systems. This will make a large proportion of the 300 000 staff who are currently employed in insurance in the UK redundant. With banking already having shed about 85 000 jobs since 1990, insurance has so far escaped unscathed.

Office staff in broking and underwriting firms will be particularly vulnerable. One United States insurer has outplaced claims handling to low wage, though highly skilled, staff in County Kerry in the Irish Republic. As soon as the communication links are in place, data handling can be performed electronically anywhere in the world.

Another challenge to the current way that insurance companies do business comes from artificial intelligence software, which mimics the human brain to make decisions in the same way as humans do, only more reliably. It can be used to detect fraud, manage and assess risk and set premiums. It threatens the traditional role of the underwriter.

Some observers argue that information age technology is replacing human beings with machines at a faster rate in the UK than elsewhere. A recent survey of managing directors from six leading industrial nations revealed that UK businesses reported more downsizing and corporate restructuring in the past two years than any other country. More than two-thirds of UK business leaders said that they expected the pace of redundancies to continue or to accelerate in the coming years.

New computer-based technologies offer a substitute for the human mind, displacing human beings with thinking machines across a wide span of economic activity. Telecommunications provides a dramatic example of wild movements in job turnover. British Telecommunications has been one of the most successful privatizations worldwide. The halving of the workforce in the last six years is seen as a major reason for that success.

A large proportion of the 1980's workforce was made up of engineers who repaired thousands of telephone exchanges scattered around the country. This was a labour-intensive activity. It doesn't happen any more because the equipment of the 1990s is computerized. It no longer has moving parts and so it doesn't need to be repaired. Telephone engineers have gone the same way as the nineteenth-century weavers.

But telecommunications has been responsible for creating new jobs too. The competition to British Telecommunications is coming from the cable companies. Cable networks are likely to cover four-fifths of the UK population by 2005. The Cable Communications Association calculates that it is creating an average of ten new jobs each working day. So there isn't a single trend in telecoms. Job losses and job creation occur simultaneously.

As well as huge changes within individual industries, there is great potential for the growth of completely new forms of employment as a result of information and communication technology. New occupations are emerging, based on information services which reinforce the creative, collaborative and social aspects of work. We shall explore these further in chapter 2.

Economists and forecasters are pinning their hopes on the knowledge sector to create new jobs. But these will be too few to absorb the millions of workers displaced by the new technologies. Knowledge by its nature needs an educated élite, not a mass labour force.

The revolution in IT has created new types of work which would have been impossible to perform five or ten years ago. The scope has increased for individuals to deliver small scale projects, generating growing opportunities to secure an income from clinching a number of contracts running side by side.

In addition to innovation in the nature of work and work contracts, new types of company are springing up which need to use people's skills in different ways from those which were more evident in the jobs for life era. As in manufacturing, changes in service industries and the growth of the knowledge sector will provide the kinds of opportunity which suit people with imagination, adaptability and drive.

The upside of downsizing

The 1980s and 1990s may have been exaggerated as the decades of delayering of managerial cadres. But they made flitting from job to job less exclusively a blue collar hazard. This experience now extends to the people who have hitherto been most secure, and able to trade on their expectation of a lifetime locked into a single career.

Many managers, professionals, administrative and technical staff have been sacrificed as companies face the pressure of global competition. The norm for an increasing proportion of companies is to employ a core of operatives and managers, with the managers finding and hanging on to the customers and the operatives serving their needs.

Others who were previously on the company payroll – designers, cleaners, lawyers, accountants, financial advisers, personnel advisers, security guards, caretakers – have ended up in a new, contract relationship, their rewards ratcheted down by the forces of competition. At the bottom of the pile are those who are too ill-educated to obtain work that gives them more than a tenuous hold on economic well-being.

For the organization, all this makes perfect sense. They have ditched the overhead costs of the accumulated rights of workers: the hidden expenses of time taken to pursue grievance and disciplinary procedures, rights to sickness absence, maternity and paternity leave, claims of unfair treatment under race, sex and disability discrimination legislation, and all the effort invested in activity that doesn't increase profitability. It makes more financial sense to release and rehire people on arm's length arrangements, making them do only the work that the company needs, instead of allowing them to pursue their own personal agendas on the company's back.

The net result is that organizations are no longer seen as providers of security of employment. The symptoms – casualization, long hours, a preference for younger workers and outsourcing – all contribute to underlying fears which grip employees all over the developed world.

However, as in other employment segments, surface developments disguise more positive trends that the career strategist can take advantage of. The key factor, as Steven Davis, John Haltiwanger and Scott Schuh have shown in *Job Creation and Destruction*, is that the flows of jobs created and destroyed in any given period are greater than the net increase or decrease in employment.

Rates of job turnover in industrial economies are surprisingly high. Figures published by the Organization for Economic

Co-operation and Development demonstrate that the total turnover or reallocation of jobs for most countries, i.e. the deletion plus creation of jobs as a proportion of the workforce, varied between 12 per cent and 20 per cent in the period from the mid-1980s to the early 1990s.

The exception was the UK, which experienced only 9 per cent turnover. But even in the UK that amounts to some two million jobs being created or destroyed on average each year. Large scale job flows are characteristic of all sectors of industry. Even declining industries are characterized by significant job turnover.

Thus around one in ten employees is likely to see their job vanishing in any year on average. This rate of turnover, with the constant interplay of defunct employment opportunities being replaced with new ones, reinforces the benefits of versatility and the possession of a range of generic skills.

We now turn to assessing your own experience and attitudes to determine whether you have, either now or potentially, the resources of personality, attitude, skills and experience to make you a natural surfer on the cross-currents of threat and opportunity generated by the tidal forces of the global market.

Activity for the global market: Are you mentally prepared to take hold of your career?

Look at the statements below. Next to each one you will find the letters A to E. For each statement, circle one of those letters according to the following key.

A True on virtually all occasions.
B True on the majority of occasions.
C True on as many occasions as it is untrue.
D Not the case on the majority of occasions.
E Not the case on virtually all occasions.

For each statement, circle the letter that most accurately reflects your attitude to the situation. For example, if your response to statement 1: "I don't apply for jobs unless circumstances force me to", is true on virtually all occasions, then circle the letter A in the adjacent column. Work through your responses quickly, without thinking for too long on each one.

ATTITUDES TO CAREER OPPORTUNITIES

1 I don't apply for jobs unless circumstances force me to.   A B C D E

2 I am willing to challenge what my boss tells me to do, if I think he or she is wrong.   A B C D E

3 I don't give up, even when I face a severe setback.   A B C D E

4 I don't mind having an uncertain future, as long as I can take the key decisions that will affect it.   A B C D E

5 If I faced a challenging deadline to complete my work, I would meet it even if it meant working all night or breaking a prearranged social engagement.   A B C D E

6 I don't change the way I set about a task, even if the way I do it doesn't seem to be effective.   A B C D E

7 If a close colleague is off work sick, I don't volunteer to cover their work.   A B C D E

8 If I'm not the leader of a team but just a member, I don't consider it my fault if the team messes up a project.   A B C D E

9 When things are going wrong, I'm the one who comes up with suggestions on how to tackle the problem differently.   A B C D E

10 I will take any genuine opportunity to extend my work-related skills, knowledge or expertise.   A B C D E

11 I don't like working in a team because I have to compromise on the way I can do things.   A B C D E

12 I will know what the signs are if I need to make a career move to another organization, in the event of the company I'm currently working for experiencing a significant downturn.   A B C D E

13 I mix easily with people.   A B C D E

14 If I come across a problem that isn't part of my professional expertise, then I hand it over to the experts rather than try to work out how to do it myself.   A B C D E

15 I keep an eye on jobs being advertised in my field of work.   A B C D E

16 I feel confident in a situation where I have to make a stream of decisions quickly, even if

some of those decisions are bound to be wrong. A B C D E

17 If I worked hard but then lost my job, I'd put it down to fate. I wouldn't believe there was much that I would have been able to do about it anyway. A B C D E

18 It takes good arguments to convince me that I'm wrong, rather than just the fact that my view is a minority one. A B C D E

19 I am aware of different salary levels that are available for the work I do, in different parts of the country and/or in different companies. A B C D E

20 When people are getting in each other's way, I'm the one who sorts them out. A B C D E

21 I don't work well unless all the conditions are right. A B C D E

22 I look out for information from non-company sources on how well the company I'm working for is doing. A B C D E

23 When it really counts, I don't take "no" for an answer. A B C D E

24 I succeed in convincing people when I set out my arguments in support of a proposal. A B C D E

25 I believe it's the company's responsibility, not mine, to offer training to improve my skills. A B C D E

26 I will say things in a way that other people find easy to understand. A B C D E

27 I am conscious of economic conditions in the area where I live. A B C D E

28 I am comfortable learning new skills and expertise through any medium, for example through attending training sessions, distance learning, independent learning, experiential learning, or using interactive technology. A B C D E

29 If my routine is disturbed, then my work deteriorates. A B C D E

30 I believe that if you take a risk that doesn't pay off, you can still be better off than if you didn't take the risk in the first place. A B C D E

31 I look for opportunities to update and extend my area of expertise. A B C D E

32 I act according to my own judgement, rather than that of other people. A B C D E

33 I believe that a risk avoided is an opportunity
   lost.   A B C D E

34 I am happy to let the organization I work for
   look after my career interests.   A B C D E

35 I'm not the one for taking on new work, if I
   do all I have to do well.   A B C D E

36 Even if other people tell me I can't achieve
   what I have set out to do, I carry on regardless. A B C D E

37 I can map out a direction for a project, and
   convince other people that this is the way to
   go.   A B C D E

38 I can present ideas clearly both orally and in
   writing.   A B C D E

39 I am happy to take on new work if I can
   learn something useful from it.   A B C D E

40 Even when I'm set a difficult task, I will
   overcome difficulties to deliver the goods.   A B C D E

41 I can make other people feel confident about
   what they are doing.   A B C D E

42 If an initiative comes unstuck, I don't believe
   I'm the one who should get it sorted out.   A B C D E

43 Given a choice between having to make a
   difficult judgement and not making one at all,
   I would still make the judgement.   A B C D E

44 I don't believe it's my job to suggest better
   ways of doing things to company managers. A B C D E

45 I don't mind being unpopular, if I know that
   what I'm doing is right.   A B C D E

46 I insist on doing things in my own way.   A B C D E

47 I would rather work out my own future than
   let the company do it for me.   A B C D E

48 If someone else is willing to take the lead in
   a project, I'm happy to let them.   A B C D E

49 I'm prepared to put up with unpopularity if
   that's the consequence of making my views
   felt.   A B C D E

50 I can get my point across effectively when I
   speak to individuals or to groups.   A B C D E

Calculating your score

This survey aims to measure your skills, knowledge and attitudes against a number of criteria which will help you to determine how ready you are to take control of your own career
strategy. Let's first of all work out your overall score. For each of
your responses, look in the appropriate column below and write
your score in the box in the right-hand column. When you have
completed your scores for all fifty statements, add them up and
complete the "total" box.

Statement no	A score	B score	C score	D score	E score	Your score
1	1	2	3	4	5	
2	5	4	3	2	1	
3	5	4	3	2	1	
4	5	4	3	2	1	
5	5	4	3	2	1	
6	1	2	3	4	5	
7	1	2	3	4	5	
8	1	2	3	4	5	
9	5	4	3	2	1	
10	5	4	3	2	1	
11	1	2	3	4	5	
12	5	4	3	2	1	
13	5	4	3	2	1	
14	1	2	3	4	5	
15	5	4	3	2	1	
16	5	4	3	2	1	
17	1	2	3	4	5	
18	5	4	3	2	1	
19	5	4	3	2	1	
20	5	4	3	2	1	
21	1	2	3	4	5	
22	5	4	3	2	1	
23	5	4	3	2	1	
24	5	4	3	2	1	
25	1	2	3	4	5	
26	5	4	3	2	1	
27	5	4	3	2	1	
28	5	4	3	2	1	
29	1	2	3	4	5	
30	5	4	3	2	1	
31	5	4	3	2	1	

32	5	4	3	2	1
33	5	4	3	2	1
34	1	2	3	4	5
35	1	2	3	4	5
36	5	4	3	2	1
37	5	4	3	2	1
38	5	4	3	2	1
39	5	4	3	2	1
40	5	4	3	2	1
41	5	4	3	2	1
42	1	2	3	4	5
43	5	4	3	2	1
44	1	2	3	4	5
45	5	4	3	2	1
46	1	2	3	4	5
47	5	4	3	2	1
48	1	2	3	4	5
49	5	4	3	2	1
50	5	4	3	2	1
Total score					

Interpreting your score

What do these results tell you about yourself?

Your score provides a guide to the sorts of skills, knowledge and attitudes that are associated with the extent to which you are willing to take control of your career. We will look at the individual components shortly, but let's first of all look at the overall impression you make.

A score of 180 or more shows someone who is very much in control and able to plan a career strategy, and to create and take advantage of career opportunities. If you score significantly over 200, then there may be an element of over-confidence. You may be prone to dismissing alternative possibilities and to closing opportunities too early. It might help you to take expert advice before pursuing your chosen course of action.

Between 140 and 180 and you're on the threshold of demonstrating the confidence, single-mindedness and determination needed to take the opportunities that arise. You are less likely, though, to be able consistently to forge new opportunities for yourself. You won't let a good chance go begging; but on the other hand you could do more to plan your future more actively.

If you scored between 100 and 140 then you incline towards caution and this will enable you to avoid rash decisions in relation to your career. But you need to be aware of the dangers of drifting. There are a number of activities in this book that will help you to broaden your outlook and to focus on alternative career directions.

Scoring under 100 leaves you vulnerable to the forces of the global market. You are trusting excessively to good fortune and need to conduct a pretty fundamental review of your own value to potential employers, especially over the longer term. You will find the next part of this activity especially valuable, as it enables you to focus on some strengths and weaknesses, thereby providing a clear agenda for prioritizing the action you need to pursue to achieve a more secure employment niche.

Let's now look at how you scored on the individual characteristics that have been the focus of this activity. Ten characteristics have been assessed on the basis of five statements associated with each characteristic. So you now need to produce a more refined set of scores from the raw material of this activity.

Individual scores against ten characteristics

We shall now separate out the five scores you achieved for each of the characteristics that have been the individual components of this activity. The characteristics were:

- determination
- flexibility
- willingness to learn
- awareness of labour market trends
- willingness to take responsibility
- initiative
- independent mindedness
- leadership
- willingness to take risks
- communication skills.

You will need to transfer the scores you gained for each of the numbered statements to the grids that are provided below.

DETERMINATION

Statement number   Your score
3
5
23
36
40
Total score:

FLEXIBILITY

Statement number   Your score
6
11
21
29
46
Total score:

WILLINGNESS TO LEARN

Statement number   Your score
10
14
28
31
39
Total score:

AWARENESS OF LABOUR MARKET TRENDS

Statement number   Your score
12
15
19
22
27
Total score:

WILLINGNESS TO TAKE RESPONSIBILITY

Statement number   Your score
8
17
25
34
48
Total score:

INITIATIVE

Statement number   Your score
1
7
35
42
44
Total score:

INDEPENDENT MINDEDNESS

Statement number   Your score
2
18
32
47
49
Total score:

LEADERSHIP

Statement number   Your score
9
20
37
41
45
Total score:

WILLINGNESS TO TAKE RISKS

Statement number   Your score

4

16

30

33

43

Total score:

COMMUNICATION SKILLS

Statement number   Your score

13

24

26

38

50

Total score:

Now transfer your score for each characteristic to the grid below.

Characteristic   Your score

Determination

Flexibility

Willingness to learn

Awareness of labour market trends

Willingness to take responsibility

Initiative

Independent mindedness

Leadership

Willingness to take risks

Communication skills

Compare the scores you achieved against each characteristic. You will see at a glance what your relative strengths are, and what you need to work on immediately to improve your all-round capacity to adopt a strategic approach to your career.

You can work on your knowledge and especially your attitudes, to make yourself more adept at meeting the challenges of the global market. If, for example, you score lower marks on initiative and leadership, look for opportunities to show those characteristics and make your own record of how you get on and what you learn from the experience. You will find that these roles come more naturally with experience.

Where you need to interact with other people, for example to show leadership skills or independence of mind, it's worthwhile to reflect upon how you behave in groups and the circumstances in which you do more than just take a back seat. Look for further opportunities to repeat that kind of experience and log the outcomes.

There are other areas where personal reflection and a willingness to change attitude can provide the motivation for more confident and assertive behaviour, for example in relation to your determination and flexibility. Look for opportunities to show these characteristics outside work by varying your routine (in relation to flexibility) or by setting yourself a target to complete a project and making sure you do it by the target date (in relation to determination). This latter feature can be exercised in the context of your leisure activities, for example.

You will also be able to improve your scores by expanding your knowledge: options include researching the local labour market and taking greater responsibility for your own learning. Don't neglect those areas where you score more highly – they may still need to be worked upon to enable you to achieve higher levels in them.

Whether or not you're happy with the score you have achieved, keep a record of it and try the questionnaire again in six or twelve months' time. This will enable you to see what dimensions have changed in the intervening period.

We will return to these characteristics in further activities that you come across in this book, to provide you with more issues to consider and act upon in order to help you to identify and take the opportunities that will undoubtedly arise as a result of the immense fluidity of organizational demand for talent, skills and expertise.

The occupational yo-yo

Look again at the score you achieved on "awareness of labour market trends", as part of the activity you have just completed. If you scored three or below, you're in good company. Few people research trends in the labour market before they set their minds on gaining entry to a particular occupation. Data is available from organizations like the Skills and Enterprise Network of the Department for Education and Employment, from local Training and Enterprise Councils and Local Enterprise Companies, and from the Institute for Employment Research.

The last of these provides a broad analysis of future trends, predicting continuing losses of jobs in these sectors in coming years:

- agriculture
- mining
- food, drink and tobacco
- textiles and clothing
- chemicals
- metals and mineral products
- engineering
- utilities (e.g. water, electricity and gas)
- transport and communications.

All these sectors have seen a decline in the number of jobs over the last quarter of a century.

The predicted growth areas are:

- distribution
- hotels
- business services
- professional services
- health
- education.

These are areas where demand has been increasing and rates of growth in productivity have been moderate. We have seen some doubts over whether distribution and banking, insurance and finance are showing signs of an interruption to the previous very rapid upward trend in employment. Even so, some increases in overall employment are predicted in these areas, as the economy grows.

In terms of the types of work people do, as opposed to the industrial sectors in which they do the work, the growth areas into the next century are predicted as being:

- managers
- administrators
- professional occupations
- personal services
- protective services
- sales.

Areas projected to decline are:

- clerical occupations
- secretarial work
- craft occupations
- plant and machine operations.

Clerical and secretarial occupations are going into reverse after a period between 1960 and 1990 when the number of jobs increased significantly. Jobs in direct production have shown a long-term tendency to decline. The economy overall is expected to provide fewer full-time manual jobs, both skilled and unskilled.

There are areas where new jobs are being created in lower-skill operations, including sales, security, cleaning and catering. But the dominant trend is for high-level skills and white collar employment (especially for women) to be favoured at the expense of low-skilled, manual jobs. An increase of about 750 000 jobs is projected for managers and administrators over the next decade. This is likely to occur despite the simultaneous delayering that's happening in many major companies.

A report produced in 1996 by the Institute for Employment Research, the *Review of the Economy and Employment: Occupational Studies*, has reinforced confidence about the importance of higher-level abilities. The demand for highly qualified people is forecast to rise rapidly, with particular demand for those with social science degrees and graduates in science and vocational subjects.

Changes in technology and the way in which work is organized have combined to favour well qualified, highly trained, white collar, non-manual activity, at the expense of poorly qualified, untrained, blue collar, manual occupations. Although there are some exceptions, this trend is likely to continue for a considerable time. Technology and globalization will jointly polarize the labour force into mobile knowledge workers gaining at the expense of immobile service workers.

It's expected that some one and a half million additional jobs for the highly qualified will be available by the year 2001, compared with 1991. However, because of the projected steep rise in the supply of graduates and other highly qualified people, there will still be a problem soaking up all those with high-level qualifications into the UK job market.

Thinking for the global market

We have seen that a general trend, either of expansion or contraction in a particular industry, can disguise undercurrents of contrary movements in the demand for labour. This is particularly the case in relation to occupational areas which are generic, as opposed to being exclusive to the industry in question. For example, there may be a greater call for salespersons for agrochemicals, at the same time as a reduction occurs in the numbers of those servicing agricultural machinery. There are profitable niches to spot in declining industries as well as in expanding ones.

As you consider the implications of new developments and contrary trends in the labour market, there will be some certainties that you can rely on to guide you through the strategies that you adopt.

- Take account of the occupational bias in favour of higher-level skills, and determine to make extending and updating your skills an integral part of your working routine.
- Invest in your own self-reliance. You can't assume that government will provide sufficiently for any point in your future.
- Interpret an investment in skills and expertise as a risk that's parallel to running your own business. Government has become less able or willing to fund education and training. Where it does come free or subsidized, we need to make the most of it. There are lots of disguised costs even in "free" education.
- Take account of demographic trends. Those which will help the young, for example, are also likely to give a new lease to the working lives of those over forty and willing to devote energy to what can still be long-term career ambitions.
- While it's easy to spot the occupations which are in decline, the UK has been poor at identifying new occupations and professions. Look out for new combinations of skills and expertise which will create fresh opportunities for those who are quick to identify them.

- Be conscious of the shelf life of the skills and expertise you
  develop, and the prospects of the industry, service or profession you enter.
- Re-evaluate the purpose of your CV. It's a document that logs
  your past. Your strategy beyond the CV needs to set out your
  agenda for the future.

The Impact of Technology

In this chapter we look at developments in technology, in order to explore the new opportunities that are coming on stream for those who are willing to use their imagination, to anticipate the future and to plan their investment in their own skills and experience accordingly.

At the centre of these developments are advances in information and communication technology. These are giving rise to new experiences which will be reflected in the way we develop our skills, organize our work and put together our employment portfolios.

There's an irony about using printed text as the medium to describe technological advance. Progress is so swift that what seems breathtaking one minute is considered commonplace the next. Even as I input the text of this book on my laptop computer, it's clear that the keyboard is archaic. Human beings are programmed to communicate by looking one another in the eye and talking – not to depress random configurations of letters on a level surface.

My purpose in surveying technological change is to stimulate you to reflect upon the implications of both the nature and the velocity of change. The career-focused activity later in this chapter will give your imagination free rein over the future, as a taster for the essential new survival skill for the next century, namely the ability to detect future directions for the shape of organizations and the structure of work.

Of course I don't pretend that I can provide comprehensive coverage of this vast subject. Nevertheless, I shall survey some key technological themes which will affect the nature of work in the years to come:

- telecommunications
- voice to text technology

- visual telecoms
- computer telephony integration
- caller line identification
- virtual reality
- the Internet
- intranets
- translation technology.

Stacks of information

In medieval times the person with access to the greatest amount of information was the Pope. His library extended to about 400 books. His librarian acted as both retrieval mechanism and regulator. The wider population only saw what the Pope wanted it to see.

The printing press introduced by Caxton in the fifteenth century created an information revolution which generated new ideas as well as widening their reach. Within the last hundred years, public libraries have created popular access to literature of all kinds. The accompanying filing and retrieval systems have brought order to huge amounts of information.

Today we have the Internet: an infinity of information with no organizing principle. Within the next few years, we will be able to acquire, on-line from our living rooms, the text of any of the twenty-four million volumes in the US Library of Congress. Five clicks of a mouse and you're down an information mine shaft with an endless labyrinth of galleries.

The Internet makes available a body of global information larger than any library one could imagine. It's also used for electronic mail allowing users to exchange messages at minimal cost. People with the ability to think beyond the confines of the orthodox are extending the horizons of this resource, by applying their imaginations to the fabrication of new applications and flights of invention.

We will always be behind the latest contrivance that these pioneers of electronic articulation devise. Nevertheless, our ambition must be to stay ahead of the thinking that organizations adopt in their wake.

Wire tapping

Peter Cochrane is head of Advanced Applications and Technologies at British Telecommunications' laboratories in East Anglia. He leads a team of 700 researchers, which aims to predict how our lifestyles will change and how this will affect telecommunications.

Cochrane uses state of the art technology to provide an environment dominated by datastreams. His car is equipped with prototype technologies that keep information flowing when he is far from his office. The telephone in Cochrane's car can call up any information he wants while he's driving: his own medical records, weather reports, news bulletins, summaries of company documents. He can have them read out to him as he drives along.

The wizardry inside Cochrane's car symbolizes the information society: the capacity to process information in any location at any time of day or night. Head working with machine to add value to some individual or organization and thereby the opportunity to create wealth.

So there are facilities coming on-stream which leave the laptop standing. The portable computer is a relatively new device but it's still pretty inconvenient. Its batteries make it heavy to handle. OK, it's smaller than a briefcase; but that doesn't stop your arms being wrenched from their sockets as you carry it around. And it's a sitting duck for any passing ethically uninhibited entrepreneur.

In ten years' time our offices will be the size of wristwatches. We will talk into them; they won't have keyboards. We'll be able to clip the electronics to our heads, mount the information onto a contact lens or a transparent sliver for a pair of glasses, or even have bits implanted. By the time the ready to wear office arrives, the way we work will have changed. Secretaries will be museum pieces. Their functions will be performed electronically.

A growing number of companies are working on producing telecoms standards that will allow users to speak to computers over the phone. This will enable activities from simple dictation to spreadsheet manipulation and database searching to occur from a remote site away from the source of information.

Elsewhere systems are being developed to lock on within instants to the information each individual is looking for. Immediately the Scott Report on the Arms to Iraq affair was published, the Labour Party (among others) used powerful software to scan and then search through the 1800 pages of text, in order to identify within a few hours the critical nuggets of information it needed in order to launch its attack on the government.

Take any text you like and a computer will be able to summarize it down to a single page. Another machine can convert the text to speech, for you to listen to wherever you happen to be. You can choose the form of input to your brain, via sound or vision, or a combination that enables you to multitask.

Our communication with machines will be increasingly through icons rather than written text. That will give us faster routes to assimilate information and new ways of learning. There is the prospect of both children and adults learning faster and retaining what they learn for longer, when they use multimedia packages rich in imagery and economical with the printed word.

This technology will drive us to become more adept at management of data from remote sites or on the move, all within breakneck timeframes. The relevant skills will break down into:

- accessing data from a range of sources
- interpreting it
- synthesizing it
- designing an appropriate multimedia mix for the finished product
- communicating it to precise target clients or audiences
- ensuring transmission ahead of competitors
- organizing the data for fast retrieval
- assessing the value of the finished product
- billing for it
- tracking the related financial transfer.

All these skills combine to form an overall talent for network management. You will have the software to deliver all these activities to speed and quality. The cerebral network inside your head will have to be wired commensurately.

Where seeing isn't believing

Videoconferencing will last longer than the keyboard. But there are limits to the value of staring into a flat screen which displays two-dimensional people. They:

- are the wrong size
- are the wrong shape

- are the wrong colour
- make sounds that come out of the wrong place
- move in a jerky, unnatural way.

You miss out on the visual cues too. Sooner or later these comic strip representations of human beings will be turned into three-dimensional representations and recreated electronically, to generate an environment that's more natural, friendly and easy to work in.

Despite the clumsiness of distance videocommunication, for many it's still a better option than endless travel. Its appeal will grow as business becomes more international, enabling the benefits of videoconferencing to outweigh the demands of travel over greater distances. Where your intelligence and knowledge are needed but your physical presence isn't, videocommunication will be sufficient. A new talent will be recognized, of making your presence felt through this two-dimensional medium.

We will see the technology improve, with video display screens the size of a wall, enabling the people at the far end of a room to appear as a literal extension of your space. Companies like Sony and Fujitsu are producing 100 inch screens at around $2 million apiece (and falling).

These and other improvements will allow the essence of physical communication to be replicated through visual technology, with sound coming from the mouth rather than side speakers, and eye contact being effected in a way that doesn't make the participant look shifty.

At the moment when you address an audience from a remote location, stress levels can rise significantly if the speaker isn't able to pick up visual cues from body language and eye contact. Distance presentations at conferences can show the speaker a hall full of people. The speaker can make out hand movements. But she or he doesn't get eye contact. That makes genuine communication very difficult, as you don't get the feedback you need to enable you to calibrate your input to the particular audience. The challenge of speaking to several audiences in different locations will require (and generate) yet more finely textured qualities of magnetism and modulation to overcome the limitations of rectangular projection.

Visual communication over distances will give rise to a demand for new skills of distance communication management. They will include:

- dress sense – with restraints on chunky jewellery that distracts or clothing (such as bold herring-bone patterns) that dazzles
- self-discipline to curb fidgety movement and other indicators of stress
- an ability to control posture and movement (e.g. keeping still when seated in a swivel chair), enabling you to reinforce your message rather than undermine it
- effective use of eye contact
- sensitivity to verbal and visual cues during discussion and negotiation
- voice modulation that reinforces your objectives.

These are all new disciplines that will have to be learnt and practised. Distance communication requires use of non-verbal skills that are of a different order from the ones that come naturally to us in face-to-face communication.

Towards the virtual workforce

Even telesales, which itself has grown significantly during the past decade, is not immune to the effects of new technology. Computer telephony integration (CTI), or screen popping, combines the functions of computer and telephone to dial customer numbers and put their details on the screen the moment the call connects. The screen displays simultaneously a script which guides the telesales staff through the conversation.

The Royal Automobile Club has installed this technology, enabling its staff to handle ninety calls a day, instead of the previous forty. At National Savings, computer telephony integration has enabled twenty-four operators to deal with an average of 144 calls a day each, compared with only 100 before its installation.

Computer telephony integration enables the computer to be used to dial numbers, route calls, and send and receive associated data. The system will soon be used beyond customer service and telesales, in administration, finance and marketing. Ovum, a London-based research company, expects the UK user figure to increase to 400 000 by the year 2000.

When this technology is used in combination with caller line identification (CLI), it becomes more powerful. Caller line identification allows the system to identify known customers as the call comes in, so that company staff can greet them by name. The system can route the call to the member of staff who dealt with them on the previous occasion, to enhance continuity.

Call centres can use information about the line number to centralize global twenty-four hour coverage, for calls from different parts of the world. Customers in individual countries are given a local freephone number to dial. As far as the caller is concerned, he or she is being dealt with by someone in their own country; but it might be somebody talking to them in their own language from the other side of the world.

Computer telephony integration also provides statistics such as length of call, length of time callers are kept waiting and number of calls relating to simple enquiries that can be handled automatically. This can impact on the planning of staffing levels. But because computer telephony integration also enables new projects to be introduced, it enhances employment prospects as often as it leads to redundancy.

The next stage of development in intelligent communication systems will take just-in-time methods to financial and service industries, with organizations using telecoms to match hour by hour fluctuations in demand with a commensurate labour supply. Take the example of betting shops.

Their busiest time of year is the fortnight prior to the Grand National. They can't afford to employ all the staff they need to take the thousands of bets they would receive if only people could get through to them. But a combination of database software, screen popping technology, expert systems and call distribution would give them access to a pool of overflow staff to enable them to expand their capacity to meet bulges in demand. All the relevant customer information can be brought up from a number of databases housed in different locations onto the operator's screen: name, account number, address, customer history and security framework. The operator's screen would itself be remote from the service company.

Those same staff could be working to several simultaneous contracts, for Marks and Spencer, Abbey National, Royal Insurance and a host of other companies. The technology will give rise to the ultimate combination of on-line, virtual workforce with portfolio worker, to generate a new breed of polycontractual worker.

Thinking for the global market

For the individual polycontractual worker, the web of employment relationships will rival the complexity of an air traffic control tower. They will find themselves contracted by one company after another, with seconds rather than months and years in between. The technology will also track each transaction, to transfer the appropriate remuneration and to generate a tamper-free efficiency report to include in the polycontractual worker's digital CV. The market for polycontractual working will increase hugely as a result.

The convergence of cheap telephone calls with the next generation of affordable parallel computers, miniaturized cameras and the digital revolution which enables words and pictures to be translated into computer code and transmitted instantly to the other side of the world will offer a riot of opportunities limited only by the vista of our imaginations.

The vision thing

In time, virtual reality will transform computers into extensions of our bodies. Virtual reality allows people to behave as if they were somewhere other than they are. That place could be the other side of the world, or an environment from hundreds or thousands of years ago, or a completely fictional recreation. Virtual reality transports perceptions by appealing to several senses at once, and by presenting images that respond immediately to your movements.

At the moment, you need to look like a begoggled freak to get the image. But as applications improve through faster and smarter computing and improved interface technology, the bulky headgear will be replaced by lightweight glasses that can superimpose synthesized images onto the real world.

People are already using multimedia applications to perform complex, delicate tasks in hazardous environments, in space for example or inside nuclear reactors. Pilots train in virtual reality cockpits that merge three-dimensional graphics with the view out of the window, and which contain sound systems that provide prompts to tell them about their surroundings. Architects can walk through the environments they are in the process of designing. Surgeons can conduct operations on a human body thousands of miles away.

As software evolves, complex systems will be reducible to models within the comprehension of human beings: global economics, viruses, galaxies, weather systems, refugee movements and so on. The capacity is immense for creating new armies of specialists to enable both expert and generalist alike to access and manipulate such applications.

Sorcerers of cyberspace

Huge numbers of organizations are attached to the Internet. All human and organizational life is there: government departments, companies, stock markets, banks, quangos, road and rail systems, air traffic control, armed forces, merchant fleets, police departments, charities, co-operatives, schools, universities, hospitals, churches, criminal organizations, political parties, world financial bodies, religious cults, the lot.

Increasingly companies are using the Internet to advertise their products and process their services. Estate agents display properties. Recruitment consultants match people to jobs. Financial service companies provide on-line quotations. Suppliers take orders and confirm delivery dates. Retailers take credit card numbers for payment.

There's no limit to what you can obtain over the Net. J.C. Keepsake Diamond in the USA offers a pledging service which generates a virtual wedding certificate after you have completed your cybervows. The service helpfully points out that the cyber-knot you tie is not legally binding. The California-based International Hedgehog Registry enables you to register for posterity all the distinguishing features of your hedgehog.

Small businesses also advertise on the Net, selling products such as smoked salmon, whisky, knitwear or restaurant meals. A European Union project provides information over the Internet for crofters who want to know when to plant their crops.

As soon as the security of systems to guarantee the integrity of cash transactions on the Internet command popular confidence, the use of the Internet for business purposes will mushroom. There are huge market opportunities for development of IT literacy among owners of small businesses. This is an area ripe for exploitation because, according to the Federation of Small Businesses, only one-third of small and medium-sized enterprises use computers at present.

The World Wide Web, the multimedia part of the Internet, had about 2000 users throughout the world in 1994. That expanded to forty million people within two years. The Web is doubling in size every three months. It is in great demand as a marketing opportunity. Many of its users are commercially attractive, high earning, technically literate males aged between twenty-five and forty, who are interested in financial services such as pensions, investments and savings. It potentially holds a gigantic market.

According to the Durlacher Multimedia consultancy's projections published in *The Internet in 1996 – an Investment Perspective*, the market in the UK is growing by more than 200 per cent a year. It's estimated that twenty-four million people could be on-line in the UK by the year 2000. By 2002, hundreds of millions of people worldwide will be connected to the Internet. The business to business area of the Internet is also growing quickly.

The Web is providing a rich seam of opportunity for companies which want to appeal to highly specialized interest groups, for example consumers who start their search for state of the art audio technology or security devices.

The opportunity-rich environment offered by the Internet is illustrated by the number of businesses established purely by chance. Mark Milmore, a Herefordshire-based etcher, set up a web page just for fun, to show some of his latest art work. Within days he was contacted by a publishing company which commissioned him to produce multimedia presentations, a computer company that wanted him to mount an exhibition for them, an American company which hired him to go to the US to do some paintings and a computer magazine that asked him to write an article. He now has his own business designing electronic pages for companies setting up websites.

Marc Andreessen, still in his twenties, became a multimillionaire when he developed one of the world's most popular Web browsers, Netscape Navigator. His was a small operation, able to be nimble-footed and to keep up with the pace of change.

Many companies use the Internet to communicate with their own staff especially if, like sales staff, they operate remotely from the company. ICL uses the Internet to provide its employees with company facts, product announcements, organizational charts, internal phone directories and case studies which recount how problems have been tackled in the past, allowing others to learn from those experiences.

Hitherto the assumption has been that new technologies are available only to well-off people. But they are also spreading to all sections of the community. For example the Samaritans' on-line service is reaching vulnerable young people through a medium that they can relate to. Homeless people in New York have been given an Internet address which has helped some of them to find a job within a month.

The Internet has become a marketing-rich environment. While users put their search engines to work to detect the precise information they're looking for, so too do owners and advertisers of websites. They're logging all the mouse clicks and key strokes in order to discover which electronic sites we visit, how long we stay there, where we have come from before and where we go to after we leave their site.

These clickstreams enjoy a digital afterlife in commercial databases. These are analysed to generate intelligence about our on-line behaviour, so that we are re-engineered into incubators of potential profit for advertisers, mass marketers and venture capitalists.

Many visitors to sites complete questionnaires and divulge personal information including name and terrestrial address, together with their views about a particular product and how the advertisements for the product affect them. All these answers go into a hopper where they're milled to add value to the corporate database of customer needs and preferences. Data mining programmes, which autonomously search data looking for group patterns, are also helpful to company sales strategies.

Internal conjunction engines

The use of intranets is also spreading. These private versions of the Internet network an individual company's computers, enabling employees to communicate and use multimedia applications in joint project work across any distance. There are thousands of intranets in use, with many more being developed.

Intranets increase access speeds and capacities above what is currently available over ordinary telephone lines. That enables users to exploit multimedia facilities of Web protocols perfected through knowledge gained from the release of prototypes on the Internet. There will also be an explosion in videoconferencing, document exchange and real-time collaborative working via intranets.

Intranets are also encouraging a switch to teleworking. What has inhibited teleworking up until now is that the information you need is usually in the wrong place – in files at the office or on somebody else's floppy disk. Intranet technology enables every PC to make its files available over the network. That will enable each worker to store all of their work in progress and their archive material, on a security-protected webserver which they will be able to access from home, from their office, or anywhere they want to.

Another development will be the increasing incidence of the twenty-four-hour world project, in which a multinational company working on research and development, product design, or any other major initiative can use its networks to progress tasks across time zones. Project teams will work in relays across the globe at the speed of daylight. The competition won't be allowed to sleep.

Among the more obvious applications are news gathering, publishing, financial dealing and information-intensive publishing, e.g. company prospectuses and reports. We can also predict a switch to cheaper labour pools around the world. It's clear that this will be another factor eroding national boundaries, as tax collectors are already finding. Notional cost centres and production centres will be located in tax-friendly areas.

Thinking for the global market

An Internet connection allows anyone to set up a virtual business and be far better informed and in touch than they could be through any other method of communication. Even the smallest company can look like a conglomerate by having an effective electronic mail service and a website.

A sound understanding of the wider applications of information and communication technology, particularly its implications for work organizations, is a precondition for security in the global market. In her book, *World Class: Thriving Locally in the Global Economy*, Rosabeth Moss Kanter argues that any small, locally based company can be successful in the global economy. She suggests that the following assets are required:

- concepts, i.e. the source of creative ideas
- competence, i.e. the ability to operate at the highest standards
- the ability to develop active global connections.

Global telecommunications and computers which can manage complex processes have brought into being the global production line. As this production line grows longer, and subdivides into more and more specialist fields, the need for new specialisms increases all the time: international accountants, lawyers, marketing professionals, management consultants, personnel professionals and so on.

It's important to keep up to date with technological developments. But it's more important to understand how these technology-driven capabilities affect business fundamentals, including:

- making sure customers are pleased with the services and products they purchase
- competing through cost and innovation
- motivating and training skilled employees.

From machine language to new age hieroglyphics

With the globalization of business, many are looking to information and communication technology to overcome the final frontier of international communication – language.

The linguistic holy grail has been to digitalize communication to enable language barriers to be overcome. Although some progress has been made with the written word, the complexity of language has prevented research and development departments from making the translator/interpreter redundant. The ability to speak several languages will, therefore, be a key business asset in the global market for decades to come.

Granted, machine-assisted translation for business already exists. The contemporary Tower of Babel, i.e. the huge building in Luxembourg which houses the European Union's translators, has software that enables a weighty document to be rendered into fairly comprehensible English inside twenty minutes. But that's a long way from the aspiration evident when Colossus cracked the Enigma code during the Second World War, that translation by machine was going to be just another code to crack.

The complexities of language, even the variables associated with a single word, are problematical. Translation software has enormous difficulty translating into French a sentence as simple as "Thank you for the fax I received yesterday". French has different words for a "fax" meaning fax machine, and "fax" meaning the message transmitted and then printed on a piece of paper. "Received" causes greater problems, given its alternative meanings of "in receipt of" and "to fence stolen goods". Translation software uses a word by word approach which, even without these problems of meaning, without human input isn't up to producing written prose that would even pass muster for a tractor operating manual.

So person to person oral communication must be relegated to the distant future as far as machine-based interpretation is concerned. There is equipment that you can speak to, which can make a fair written representation of what you've said (in the same language). And there are machines that can convert written text to spoken language. So the rudiments have been developed. But that's a long way even from approximate interpretation, let alone spontaneous conversational real-time translation.

At the same time the information age is reconstructing the concept of literacy. While currently it means the ability to read and write, in the digital age it will mean the ability to understand information, however it is presented.

Increasingly information is being packaged in new ways. The monopoly of black letters printed on a white page is ending. New formats blend words with recorded sound and images into rich and fluid combinations. This new mix – known as multimedia – can be reformatted, rescaled and transformed, to create an imagery appropriate to the objective.

Digital literacy will make new demands of employees and portfolio workers. But there isn't a generation of teachers or lecturers in being to impart the associated skills. Some consider this an advantage, as digital literacy is a medium in which you learn by experimentation and being in control. The information society trades in digital goods. Digitally literate individuals will be among those who derive their wealth from the information age.

Thinking for the global market

It's difficult to foretell precisely what the new areas of work arising from advances in information and communication technology will be. And no sooner will one appear than it will mutate into several derivatives.

Nevertheless it is feasible to begin to map out the kinds of areas which will give rise to new income streams. We have already seen how the just-in-time approach will impact upon service areas.

Another area of innovation will be the customized production line which will enable the client to specify down to fine detail the features they want on their car, their clavichord, their TV viewing or their on-line "newspaper".

And the kind of new work that the demands of customization will give rise to are in the area of logistics – organizing the supply of resources, their delivery and assembly in optimal fashion to produce a host of tailored packages at lowest cost.

Another area ripe for development is networking and consultancy services associated with the formation and reformation of virtual companies. With an increasing tendency for companies to come together for very short periods, and to be run by people who never meet in person, there will be a need for constant logistical support to ensure that the various stakeholders in these alliances are compatible, and that they coalesce and dissolve cleanly, avoiding high transactional costs.

There will also be new business generated almost by accident, as we discover that ideas which appear to have no intrinsic appeal catch on universally despite the combined wisdom of orthodox experts. Take going to the doctor's surgery as an example. Who for a minute would imagine that a patient who is sick would be satisfied with a visit to the surgery that involved interfacing with a machine rather than having a personal consultation with a doctor?

Yet research has shown that men, especially, are reluctant to go to a doctor even if they're convinced they have something wrong with them. There's a significant volume of people who would prefer to go through a diagnostic trail with a computer, pointing to the location of their pain via a diagram on a screen, thereby avoiding the embarrassment of using words to tell a doctor the same thing.

Will that put the general practitioner out of work? Clearly not. But it will provide sources of new types of work for researchers, software designers, promoters, sales people and others.

Another area ripe for exploitation is niche communication, in an endless variety of human contexts. Let's take education as an example.

Most of those involved in education argue that there's no substitute for putting a teacher or lecturer in front of a class. But that view is untenable in the long term. Is the serious learner really going to put up with the untested local teacher when he or she can have a learning package delivered by a natural communicator with whom the technology allows them to interact?

The multimedia stars of the future are as likely to be teachers as rock guitarists. Sure there will be local tutorial groups to enable students with common learning programmes to spark off one another, with the help of a local tutor. But there are now people studying chemistry or law who might not be particularly gifted in those subjects, but who nevertheless will become mass communicators for their chosen field of study. These will be among the new generation of niche communicators – media stars performing to the expectations of select coteries of devotees.

Activity for the global market: Exploring mutations in the organization of work

We have just looked at an example of an opportunity that will arise in the field of education as a result of the impact of technology on the organization of learning. An educationist with the qualities of drive, determination and the requisite communication skills might decide to draw up a self-investment and networking programme in order to be in a position to take advantage of that opportunity.

Which factor will be most critical to the success of such a venture? Being the best communicator? Having the deepest knowledge of the subject area? I would argue not. A degree of talent is necessary of course, as is a sound grasp of the subject matter to be communicated to the wider learning audience. But the most significant factor in determining success will be how early one gets into the market with the appropriate skills.

This is because it's rarely the best product or service that dominates the market. Rather, it's the one that catches on the fastest. In the early days of product development, it's most often the package that reaches the market first that becomes the leader.

Hence the value of developing a mindset that enables you to anticipate and prepare for trends in your area of expertise. Surprisingly perhaps, very few people ask themselves what will happen to the form of paid activity that they're currently engaged in over the next few years.

True, we speculate about whether our current job will last, whether we will be victims of downsizing and so on. But most of us don't reflect upon the questions that would lead us to the more reliable conclusions we need in order to plan the kinds of investment in our own skills and expertise that will enable us to take advantage of openings in the global labour market.

So the next activity will provide a focus on the kind of thinking that will enable us to diagnose trends early enough to take advantage of them. We take as our baseline, some predictions about our future, which British Telecommunications publishes and updates regularly on the Internet.

We have already come across British Telecommunications' research team devoted to predicting how life will change in the coming decades. Many other organizations are engaged in the same line of business, but British Telecommunications just happens to put a selection of their material onto the Internet. So let's take as our prompt, their assessment of the shape of life to come.

The object of the activity is to focus our thinking on the implications of social, economic and technological developments for the future of work. It doesn't matter whether specific predictions come true or not.

The British Telecommunications research team formats its predictions in the form of a calendar which sets out:

- the earliest date that the team believe a specific development is feasible
- the most likely date
- the latest possible date.

We will take the most likely dates from the alternatives they provide. Here are some examples.

Date	Prediction
2000	Production of hand videophones
	Availability of voice-based telephone connection
2005	Availability of personal, wearable health monitor
	Entire human DNA sequence mapped out
	Development of computers which write their own software.
	Production of domestic robots
	Availability of machines operated entirely through voice interaction
2007	Operation of totally automated factories
2010	Development of artificial heart
	Introduction of universal identity cards
2015	Availability of near-Earth space tours
2016	Development of neuro computers
	Availability of robots to undertake security patrols of buildings
2020	Average life span will be 100 years.

Let's choose some of the more plausible predictions and reflect upon what the implications might be for the future of employment against four dimensions:

- global
- national
- local
- your own employment environment.

Naturally in the examples that follow, I can't assess the implications of these predictions for your particular working environment. So I shall use, as an illustration, someone with a job as a personnel manager in the retail trade.

Here's the first example: "production of hand videophones". Add to the predictions provided below your own assessment of how the working environment will be affected by the availability of hand videophones. Allocate your predictions to each of the four dimensions we have identified.

**PREDICTIONS FOR WORK CONSEQUENCES OF
PRODUCTION OF HAND VIDEOPHONES**

Implications for work globally

- Expect peaks and troughs in the flow of incoming international calls consistent with time zone differences.
- Organize outgoing international calls in batches after you have spruced up your physical appearance.
- Be ready to pick up cues about cultural and personal background of new contact on videophone, e.g. ethnic profile, age, status.
- Arrange physical appearance of working environment to enhance global image of organization.
- Use visual cues (e.g. weather, location) to establish rapport before launching into business content of call.
-

Implications for work in the UK

- Organize outgoing calls in batches after you have spruced up your physical appearance.
- Pressure to allocate named employee to each client, to reinforce personal nature of service.
- Implications for training each employee to be able to deal comprehensively with all the needs of each individual client.
- Implications for breadth, flexibility and knowledge base of each employee.
- Closer attention to background features of working environment, e.g. outlawing of visual material in poor taste.
-

-
-
-
-

- Introduction of new disciplines for home-based employees, to ensure they present a businesslike image.
- Gain clues about cultural and social values and expectations when making a new contact by videophone, e.g. ethnic background, age, status within the organization.
- Arrange physical appearance of working environment to enhance public image of organization.
-
-

Implications for work locally

- Closer attention to background features of working environment, e.g. outlawing of visual material in poor taste.
- Introduction of new disciplines for home based employees, to ensure they present a businesslike image.
-
-
-
-
-
-

Implications for my own work context (e.g. personnel role in retail)

- Introduction of safeguards against recruitment practices which discriminate on grounds of appearance.
- Introduction of work disciplines to ensure that videocalls are not subject to interruption by casual callers.
- Provision of training to enable employees to use videophones with confidence.
- Establishment of systems which record which employee dealt with each customer, so that the relevant employee can be given responsibility for follow-up calls, in line with customer expectations.
-
-

What do we notice from this first example? Here are some pointers.

- Some of the implications are similar for the various dimensions.
- Other implications might not impact at all against more than a single dimension.
- Some of the implications for the work environment must be speculative because they are subject to large numbers of variables.
- Some developments may affect the way in which work is done (e.g. need to prepare physical appearance to convey positive company image), but without any measurable impact – either positive or negative – on continuity of employment.

We can now work on another example, but this time fill in your own responses to all the predictions, including "implications for my own work context", on the basis of your current employment or earning situation. Two examples are provided in each of the "global", "UK" and "local" boxes. We will take one of the British Telecommunications predictions for 2005: "availability of machines operated entirely through voice interaction".

AVAILABILITY OF MACHINES OPERATED ENTIRELY THROUGH VOICE INTERACTION

Implications for work globally

- Global domination of a small number of machine interface languages, including English and Spanish, and consequent need to reach sufficient levels for interaction with local machinery
- Remote interaction with machinery
-
-
-
-

Implications for work in the UK

- Growing competition for remote machine interface jobs from overseas applicants able to speak English
- Intense competition for share of the interactive voice-machine equipment and software market
-
-
-
-

Implications for work locally

- Sudden decline of industrial centres and growth of unemployment blackspots
- Corresponding growth in some centres of population through inward investment
-

Implications for my own work context

-
-
-
-
-

Next choose two of the British Telecommunications predictions (or two other developments you are aware of) which are likely to have the greatest impact on your work and assess their implications in the same way.

PREDICTION 1:

-

Implications for work globally

-
-
-
-
-

Implications for work locally

-
-
-
-
-
-

Implications for work in the UK

-
-
-
-
-

Implications for my own work context

-
-
-
-
-
-

Now choose your second prediction and complete the activity in the same way.

PREDICTION 2:

-

Implications for work globally

-
-
-
-
-

Implications for work locally

-
-
-
-
-
-

Implications for work in the UK

-
-
-
-
-

Implications for my own work context

-
-
-
-
-
-

Feedback

Now a few conclusions from the activity we have completed and some suggestions for follow-up activity. First of all let's not underestimate the difficulty of the exercise. It really doesn't matter whether our assessments of the implications of the British Tele-communications predictions actually come about or not. There are enough research teams in the UK and around the globe to worry about the accuracy of their own predictions.

The point of this exercise is to have you reflecting routinely on the nature of your work and employment contract, so that when you come across or read about developments either inside your own field of work or outside it, your mind is ready to think through the implications for your own future earning prospects.

More often than not, the implications of a particular develop-ment you come across will be negligible, or will have no bearing at all on the nature of the work you do. But just occasionally there will be a trend or event or technological advance which will have a significant impact.

Working out the nature of the likely effects will be much easier than the exercise you have just completed. Take the example of attacks on schoolchildren in Dunblane and Wolverhampton in 1996. Tragic as these incidents were, they resulted (quite under-standably and with the vigorous support of parents) in new oppor-tunities for security firms.

The ones that benefited were those which were geared up to fit devices to schools throughout the country, as public concern about school safety heightened and government provided an injec-tion of funding to support schools in their endeavours to ensure that similar tragedies did not recur.

As a follow-up to this activity then, look out for developments that might affect the area of economic activity that you're engaged in. Apply the exercise to those developments. Then, after six months or so, reconsider your responses and decide whether you still agree with what you have written or whether you would respond differently.

If you repeat the exercise periodically, you will develop a frame of mind in which you are constantly assessing the implications of changes in society, in the economy and in science and tech-nology, and applying the lessons you learn to your investment in the development of your skills, knowledge, experience and expertise.

The location of the British Telecommunications Laboratories website which includes the calendar of predictions is provided in References and Further Reading at the end of this book. Keep looking at this website for updates, and repeat this exercise on the basis of what you find there.

Thinking for the global market

Developments in technology are being applied to work organizations at an accelerating rate. We need to keep up to date with those advances which affect our area of work, and to anticipate their consequences. There's some follow-up work to be accomplished too, as indicated below.

- When you spot a new development, it's unlikely that appropriate training will be immediately available, as it takes time for the training industry to catch up. But you can look for analogous training. For example, you can get up to speed with the disciplines associated with videoconferencing, by undertaking media training which is usually aimed at public relations officers.
- Keep up to date with technological developments by reading the innovation pages in the newspapers and subscribing to specialist publications like *New Scientist* and *Management Today*.
- When you're entering a new work contract or making an employment move, stress your commitment to self-investment in horizon skills, i.e. those competences associated with new technology such as delivering presentations at a distance. By doing so, you will demonstrate to a prospective new employer not only that you're pursuing state of the art human resource investment, but also that you're already thinking ahead for the benefit of his or her company.
- Think of your own self-development as an equivalent investment to purchasing a property: the value of your investment can go down as well as up. By being well informed about developments that are likely to affect your area of work, you will minimize the risks associated with investing in yourself. Your optimum source of long-term security is inside your head.

3

Attitudes to Work

Since the rise of Protestantism and the development of early modern capitalism in the sixteenth century, success has been a male-defined and male-orientated concept associated with calling, vocation or career. The small number of options earmarked in the past for women aspiring to recognition, like heiress or witch, have had their drawbacks.

However, the late twentieth century has seen the cosy citadels of professionals besieged and the rungs of organization based career ladders sawn through. As a consequence, men have been forced to reassess the foundations of their heavily skewed social identities.

Jonathan Gershuny of Essex University has demonstrated that those with the highest monthly incomes work the longest hours and have the least time to spend it. They also have less opportunity to see to their other responsibilities and needs. Income rich equals time poor.

At the same time dual career partnerships have deprived men of the ministrations of the traditional "wifey-at-home" which used to be the mainstay of their success. Gone too is the uxorious unctuousness that was once an obligatory feature of the end-of-career eulogy. The notion of success as the single-minded pursuit of power, wealth and position based on a gender specific division of labour, has its days numbered. Different models are springing up ready to take its place.

We need more research before we can quantify which post-industrial work attitudes will become dominant. Among the questions that need to be answered are:

- What forms do current psychological contracts within the work environment take?
- What happens to people forced out of high-flying entrepreneurial roles?

- Do they downshift willingly?
- Are they permanent casualties?
- Do they reappear in similar roles in other organizations?
- Do they call it a day and spend the rest of their days in a Mediterranean villa?
- Do they become local councillors or find some other form of life outside work?
- Might they rediscover (or just discover) what's involved in a personal relationship?
- What happens to those who stay in organizations?
- Do they work ever longer hours?
- Are they more loyal or less?
- Do they become more resentful and subversive?
- How secure do they feel?
- Do they develop career defences to enable them to survive (economically at least) the threat of redundancy?
- Can they even dare to divulge their alternative career strategies to their bosses, for fear of giving out the message that the company isn't the unalloyed focus of their waking lives or might not be in future?

Working out the cost of living

These questions relating to post-industrial work attitudes are being addressed by management academics. They are areas of research which would have been considered eccentric even ten years ago. Now they presage the beginnings of a counter-offensive on the part of increasing numbers of employees who are looking for a relationship with their company in which servility and dependence are replaced by mutual respect achieved through a psychological contract based on equity.

One front-running alternative to being indentured to a wholesale company lifestyle is the concept of the life–work balance. This is often characterized as a "feminine" solution because it challenges the stereotype of the corporate executive, for whom concern for non-work-related responsibilities would earn a high wimp rating.

One source of the life–work balance concept is, of course, disillusionment with the excessive demands of corporate life. Judi Marshall of the Bath University School of Management has found a trend for significant numbers of women in top corporate jobs to give up under organizational pressures.

Marshall (1996) interviewed sixteen female managers who had decided to leave work for reasons other than career progression and her results are published in her book, *Women Managers Moving on: Exploring Career and Life Choices*. These managers left their organizations because of:

- their desire to create a lifestyle not dominated by work
- the difficulty they experienced in working within an environment characterized by office politics, bullying and aggression
- exclusion from decision making
- having their performance judged according to "masculine" stereotypes
- the discovery that their management roles required them to behave in ways that were alien to their natural dispositions.

It's not only women, though, who feel uncomfortable with the excesses of corporate fundamentalism. My own research for this book has elicited a depth of concern on the part of male as well as female respondents from a variety of organizational backgrounds.

Graham Whitehead, advanced concepts manager at British Telecommunications, puts the contrast at its starkest, between "those who are working ever longer hours, and those who aren't working at all. I can see that a lot of people who are currently working very long hours will die prematurely. They will get to the point that they just can't cope any more." This perception struck a chord with some of my other witnesses, who saw evidence of managers working harder than ever because of their fears for the future.

Philip Morgan, who has worked in a multinational environment for the past ten years, recalls a period when the organization he then worked for:

> was making a lot of people redundant and everybody I knew was calculating what their redundancy benefit would be every couple of weeks. We were all very insecure. And the company was happy to exploit the psychological pressure for us all to work long hours. And even then it didn't make much difference and they got rid of a lot of people.

Morgan accepts the inevitability of the resulting resentment against the company, and even a feeling of wanting to retaliate. But for the time being at least he needed to maintain his commitment to a corporate career. "But there's no sense of loyalty – in either direction. I know they'll ditch me if they have to, so I need to make some contingency plans."

Morgan's sense of insecurity is shared by many others pursuing corporate careers. However, their fears are contradicted by the evidence of national data series like the *Labour Force Survey*. This shows remarkable consistency over several decades in rates of job turnover and in the length of the average period in employment.

Nevertheless, to so many people working for organizations, the insecurity is tangible. In addition to work-related pressures, developments in society are also responsible for creating a renewed demand for a life–work balance. One aspect of the debate about the potential excesses of the work "ethic" is whether people are willing to trade material reward for more time to invest in their families and personal relationships, their leisure pursuits, their existence outside work.

Social pressures are creating as severe a squeeze on individuals' time as work pressures. Divorce can make intensive demands as more time needs to be invested to compensate the children of a downsized partnership. Children of a new partner can create demands, as well as children of the new relationship. There might also be elderly parents who, if they too have split up, double the time commitment in terms of visits.

The company executive might try to buy their way out of trouble by hiring nannies and paying fees for residential education. But these are no substitutes for the emotional investment that close ones need. If both partners are working, the juggling of caring responsibilities can cause stress to both partners.

Many of the most gifted who are in full-time work have no time for anything or anyone but themselves and their work. They have to be totally immersed in their organizations to succeed. That doesn't do them any good. It's questionable whether the organization they work for gains as a result either – or their clients, as a patient operated on by a junior hospital surgeon towards the end of a long shift might discover . . .

Some observers have found worrying signs of what's happening to people inside work organizations. As a result of increased competition both between and within companies, people are driven by rapid reaction communication systems and the demands of worldwide computer networks to process ever-increasing volumes of work.

The result is evident in many workplaces: shrinking attention span, reduction of working memory, behavioural dislocation, weakening of deductive thought and an increasing search for compensation through litigation.

Starting prices for a new generation

As more people are displaced from full-time work, with empty time on their hands and unused potential in their heads, a new generation is coming onto the upper end of the labour market aware of the pitfalls of short-termism and wrong turnings. They are looking for signposts to enable them to find their way in an increasingly bewildering work environment.

Mike Jennings, recruitment manager for Price Waterhouse, has detected a willingness among more able students to forgo initial rewards, and instead to opt for the more valuable long-term investment of training and relevant experience. A recent Universum International study found that salary was only the twelfth most important benefit among European students' rankings.

Michal Kalinowski, president of Universum International, finds top students looking for dynamic organizations which give them responsibility for running their own projects. They're also looking to work for companies open to new ideas.

Colm Tobin, careers specialist at University College Dublin, has noticed that graduates are looking to the long or medium term, with less concern about initial salary levels. "Most have a long fuse. After a couple of years they can start to compare themselves and benchmark against others in the same industry."

In the 1980s many looking for their first job wanted a big starting salary and car. Now high flyers are more horizon minded, placing greater importance on development of their skills and social networks, and often on the chance to work in a talented multicultural team. Those whose abilities are in demand can exploit their rarity value and secure further investment in their career development.

There is also greater recognition that knowledge- and fact-based competence are less important than flexibility. This has prompted many to look for companies that can offer them the opportunities to acquire new skills as an investment in their future employability.

These young high flyers are less likely to be loyal to a single company. They know that their current body of knowledge will become redundant sooner rather than later, and so will need to broaden their experience through working for a variety of employers.

Chris Brewster, director of the Centre for European Human Resource Management at Cranfield University, agrees that people are beginning to understand what's happening and that young people are not looking for a long-term career in a single company any longer. He is less convinced, though, that people are working out their moves much further than their first or next job.

Another consideration is that graduates often start their careers in debt, and that can make starting salary significant. Jonathan Bratt, global account director at A.C. Nielsen, which specializes in marketing research, doesn't believe that negotiating a high starting salary is the prime objective of anyone interested in a long-term career. He has also detected a fatalistic attitude to redundancy among contemporaries who have already embarked on a corporate career: "if it happens, it happens".

Coming back to life

Other researchers have detected new thinking among younger entrants to the labour market in response to the pressures of modern working life. Stephen Perkins, director of the Strategic Remuneration Research Centre, for example, has noticed that young people have seen what happened to their parents and don't want the baggage that comes with working for big companies.

Investigations by the European think tank, Demos, conclude that eighteen to thirty-four year olds are much less committed to the idea of a regular job than older people. *Generation X and the New Work Ethic* concludes that this age group are more concerned with developing a portfolio of interests and useful skills, than in a job for life.

Some management thinkers are encouraging greater assertiveness among high flying executives. Reggie von Zugbach, professor of management at Paisley University, in his book *The Winning Manager*, argues that people in work are right to be paranoid about organizations.

Von Zugbach describes companies as enemies to be despised. He urges executives to take charge of their own destiny and suggests that employees should only take advantage of company-sponsored training if it genuinely contributes to their own

development. He urges them to avoid the propaganda-based
instruction which often masquerades as training.

Philip Morgan, now ten years into his corporate career, is aware
that he will soon need to make some critical decisions about the
direction he wants to take.

> Your early to mid-thirties is when you really accelerate
> in your career (if you're going to). But at that point I
> won't necessarily want to go any further, because of the
> sacrifice in terms of the absolute commitment that that
> would require. I'd even be prepared to downshift in
> order to be able to pursue my interests outside work.

He has also worked out his contingency plans for maintaining
his income if he were made redundant. He has researched the
requirements and costs of retraining as a lawyer and worked out
the options with his partner, who is also pursuing a long-term
career strategy. Morgan has also persuaded his current company
to invest in the skill areas he would need if he were to go it alone
– though he has thought better of sharing his motivation with
them. Another element of his bail-out plan is the network of
contacts he is assiduously building up, especially when he travels
overseas.

Morgan stresses the benefits of a survival strategy. "One, if the
worst happens you're prepared. Two, if the worst doesn't happen,
you're still in a better position to take advantage of opportunities that arise in your company."

Alex Rink, now in his late twenties and with experience in
automotive manufacture and logistics, is determined to avoid
becoming dependent upon a single company.

> I've seen enough of people in their fifties who believed
> that working for a single company for an extended
> period of time would serve them well. Then, the next
> thing they know is that they've been laid off and they
> just don't seem to know what they're going to do with
> their lives. What most companies do not seem to realize
> is that by downsizing and firing people, they are encour-
> aging self-reliance and independence on the part of their
> employees.

Rink sees the most effective approach as "being your own company", as he views his fundamental source of security as being
derived not from his employer but from his own independence

and self-reliance. "My career strategy is to gain as many skills, and as much knowledge and international experience as I can to ensure that I never become entirely dependent upon any one company."

Yvonne Baker, international sales manager for a multinational with its headquarters in Canada, is conscious of the trapdoor nature of organizational employment. "At the moment I'm doing very well for my company. But it only needs a new boss to come in who perhaps I don't get on with; or a merger that means I'm not needed any more. My fall-back is to make sure I'm mobile."

Richard Steele, who is taking a year out from management consultancy to study at the INSEAD business school at Fontainebleau, is convinced that his generation has taken on the career reality of working for several organizations – not only in succession, but simultaneously too in some circumstances.

> People now expect to be selfish and to move to their own benefit between organizations in a sort of mercenary manner, because organizations no longer give you the loyalty that they used to. We expect to be unemployed for periods, or to be forced to switch jobs. We accept that we have to rely on our own initiative, unlike our parents' generation who just joined an organization and stayed with it.

But it's not all one-way traffic either. Abbi Wilson, currently freelance but with a track record in training in France and the UK, is now intent on making the return journey back to an organizational career. She will miss the variety and freedom of portfolio working. But she's resigned to participating in the politics of corporate life and to the organizational expectation that places a higher priority on attendance at work than on the added value that an employee will earn for the company.

Coming to a head: Debra Hawkins

Debra Hawkins is European sales manager for the robotics division of a multinational conglomerate. Her company sponsored her to study for an MBA. After she had started the degree, they asked her to commit herself to staying with the company for four years after completion of the degree.

Hawkins felt this should have been raised with her before she embarked upon her studies. She wanted to object, but concluded that the company had the upper hand: if she made too much fuss, they would think of her as not being committed to the company.

She asked around her peers and found that a demand for such an undertaking was unprecedented. She then tried to negotiate a reciprocal pledge from the company to herself, i.e. that the company would guarantee employment for her for at least four years. The company refused. Hawkins decided to accept the position nevertheless.

Reasserting control: Rachel Tyson

Rachel Tyson began her career in London as a legal secretary. She studied law in her spare time. From there, she worked in advertising for three years and then went into estate agency.

She spent some time working freelance, securing successive contracts from large organizations in management consultancy. This was followed by a period employed in the sales division of a large electronics company.

Tyson eventually turned against the accumulated pressure and moved to France, where she now makes an income from a range of activities from writing to decorating. Her decision to exchange a high level of income for control over her life was deliberate and calculated. She sees the loss of income as the only drawback.

> All my energy was expended for the sake of the company who, in exchange, paid me vast amounts of money. However, it occurred to me that what they were paying for was my life and it was passing by without any real achievement.
>
> Now, I have to achieve in order to live. One of the greatest advantages of my lifestyle is that it's my own strengths and weaknesses that determine the quality of my life. If I want something, it's not merely a question of walking down to the shops to get it. I have to work out how to achieve it without the aid of a large bank account. So I rely on my survival instinct, rather than on my bank balance.
>
> I don't work to deadlines. My mind isn't stretched to breaking point with financial decisions. Instead, it's stretched as far as my own imagination can take it. I now

decide my own priorities, rather than setting goals for the profit of an organization that could easily replace me.

I'll never move back to working for a large organization. They can't afford to pay me what my life is worth and I'm not prepared to prostitute my thinking power any longer. I'm stronger now than I've ever been, because surviving here in Brittany has taught me that I have the freedom to choose how I spend my days, rather than being an exhausted shell of a person, too tired to use my imagination.

The key factors for this total change of lifestyle are people's capabilities, their strength of character and their flexibility.

Thinking for the global market

Debra Hawkins was clearly a high flyer within her company, selected for special investment by them. But her experience illustrates how even someone in a strong bargaining position was unable to persuade her company to accept an arrangement other than on its own terms.

Rachel Tyson took a deep, hard look at how she was spending her life and made some fundamental decisions on what to change and how to change it. You need to consider the options and work out what kind of strategy is the best for you.

- Are you ready to give up your corporate existence in the Rachel Tyson mould?
- Are your long-term interests still better served through working for an organization?
- If you are still committed to an organization but are working on an alternative future, do you kiss and tell?
- Or do you keep your own counsel?
- How favourably do you expect your employer to respond if you tell her or him that in the global economy, loyalty is a redundant commodity on both sides of the employment contract?
- How will your employer view you if you're explicit in asking for support to invest in your skills, as preparation for the inevitable parting of the ways?

Much of the private sector still exhibits a culture reminiscent of the football transfer market. If you tell the manager you're interested in joining another side, you can find yourself in the reserves or packing your bags. Protocol still ensures that employee references are rarely requested *before* you've been offered a new job.

Nevertheless there's growing recognition in some firms of the mutual benefit of investing in the employee's long-term career, even if that takes him or her out of the company. Hence the growth of well-resourced open learning centres in companies like Vauxhall and Ford.

Increasingly employers are adopting the Investors in People standard. As its name suggests, Investors in People requires a commitment by employers to invest in the training and skills of their employees. Over 50 per cent of organizations with more than 200 employees are now committed to meeting the standard. The scheme does, though, place a higher priority on training and development geared towards company targets in preference to the employee's own development objectives.

Nevertheless, contributing to the employee's long-term needs is becoming part of the new contract between the employer and the employee, particularly in circumstances where long-term job security cannot be guaranteed. Today's organizations can no longer demand the undying loyalty of their staff. They have to earn that kind of commitment.

Conscious of the fluidity of the labour market, Abbey National has introduced personal development diaries on behalf of its employees. More than 6000 have been requested, even though their use is optional among the workforce. The company's objective is to help individuals think through career options for themselves.

Organizations adopt a range of stances on individual career development. One school of thought is to develop careers in line with the organization's business needs. This is a narrow approach, which ties the individual to the organization's priorities rather than their own. At the other extreme is the school of self-managed careers. This relies on development being undertaken by individuals who want to maintain their external employability.

A third group combines the two, through an understanding that a flexible company requires the entire workforce to be adaptable to continuous change. It focuses on the career as less of an upward progression than a series of role adaptations arising from project team working and lateral job movement. This is more of a partnership approach. Organizations such as British Petroleum, Norwich Union and British Telecommunications are adopting this approach.

In her book *Strike a New Career Deal*, Carole Pemberton explores how trade-offs can be made between the company and the individual. She argues the value of negotiating a sequence of specific deals, to meet both the requirements of the organization and the individual's need to be employable in the longer term. For instance an individual can seek greater work variety as part of an investment in his or her career; the employer benefits commensurately from the broader contribution made to the business. Many companies expect the individual to take the initiative in proposing such a deal.

From the organization's point of view, there's much to be gained from meeting people half way in their career development and finding creative ways of accommodating their life and career goals, not least retention of staff with initiative and energy.

Many companies share with their employees a deep sense of unease about the future. In organizations where the boundaries of traditional jobs are crumbling, where careers are self-managed and where the individual knows his or her own worth, companies are finding themselves subject to the same uncertainty as their workforce, unable to rely on traditional values of loyalty and commitment.

Some employers are counteracting this volatility of labour by offering development opportunities tailored to the demands of each individual employee. This is a strategy that can overcome the perennial doubts that many employees express: if the company can no longer offer me a career, a pension or a safe job, then what am I doing here?

Denise Lincoln, human resources director of Allied Domecq, sees the beginnings of a change in company attitudes. "I suppose it depends on the company. I think in the majority of situations people would admire the initiative and it would be rewarded. It's certainly an indictment if companies don't know what their employees' aspirations are or if they don't make a genuine effort to support them."

Many international companies now make it clear that they don't expect a lasting relationship with their new recruits, and this makes it easier for employees to negotiate a self-investment package without suffering a backlash from the company. A number of banks, for example, offer a two-year associateship, with no commitment beyond that.

Tony Webb, director of education for the Confederation of British Industry, has also detected a greater willingness among companies to earn employee loyalty by ensuring that their skills are updated, sometimes beyond the immediate requirements of the business, thereby helping to ensure that their employees maintain their value in the labour market.

> Lots of organizations that have downsized have been only too eager to help employees acquire additional skills. They know they won't be able to offer their employees a job for ever. So by helping them enhance their skills, they're more likely to find employment opportunity when the time comes to say goodbye.

David Taylor, employment development manager at Anglian Water, encourages employees to declare their desire to invest in their long-term career even if that is likely to be outside the company. This extends to encouraging people to acquire skills through voluntary work, for example as a local government councillor or a magistrate.

> We recognize that people will find change easier if they are more confident about their abilities. I think there's a growing awareness among UK employers that we need to encourage people to take a broader view of their lives and that you'll get a better payback to the company if you do that.

Graham Whitehead, advanced concepts manager at British Telecommunications, is full of enthusiasm for an open discussion with the employer about employability. He classes his own company as one of the more enlightened, saying, "What we can give you in return for loyalty is not a job for life, but to make you more employable for your next job."

It's important, though, not to paint too rosy a picture of the general level of support for self-investment. UK plc didn't get where it is now on the basis of an angelic host of altruistic employers seeing to the long-term interests of their employees before even considering any other priorities.

Some of the people I interviewed were sceptical about the willingness of their employers to take anything other than a narrow view of employee self-development. They also explained their frustration at not being able to be honest with their employers, and argued how counterproductive this was to the interests of the company as well as the employee.

The ambiguity evident on the issue of self-investment reinforces the need to research the company you're interested in before you agree to a new contract. The multinational and larger national companies are warming in their attitudes to the concept of a psychological contract which accepts the legitimacy of the employee preparing for a career outside the organization.

It will, though, take some time before this more enlightened view is accepted universally. You will need to assess where the balance of advantage lies if you're considering accepting a contract with a company that doesn't yet understand this implication of the new work order.

Collectors' items

The starkest alternative to pursuit of a corporate career with a single organization is the adoption of a magpie approach to securing an income, by running a clutch of contracts side by side. Part of the attraction is the ability to weave non-work and social priorities into a complete life package.

The move towards flexible working will reinforce the opportunities for portfolio workers to pursue contracts on the basis of a personal menu that might include:

* evening work
* term-time jobs
* weekend projects
* annualized hours
* nine-day fortnights
* defined output contracts
* single-hour contracts (grossed up).

For increasing numbers of people, portfolio working provides an attractive alternative to "secure" or "permanent" employment. It cuts out regular commuting, office politics, the promotion rat race and attendance at a work base for its own sake. It can generate a basic income from fewer than five or six days a week, and enable participants to pursue their own projects in the additional time they reserve for themselves.

Portfolio workers don't suffer from the implicit blackmail of the threat of delayering, thereby being forced to spend almost every waking hour on the losing side of the psychological contract with the organization. It's also easier for both partners within a relationship to pursue their careers independently and to share their caring responsibilities more equitably.

That doesn't make portfolio working an unblemished new age idyll. There are disciplines to adhere to, such as doing the accounts, chasing up bad debts, pitching for work and being obliged to ensure that any periods of sickness don't compromise the needs of the customer. It is risk laden and prone to generate stress. You have to commit yourself, no less than in a corporate career, to investing in your own skills to keep up with the changing nature of the market you're involved in.

More people are considering portfolio working as a lifetime career option. Many will gain vicarious experience of elements of portfolio working even when employed full time by companies, as the organization of work in those companies changes and replicates some of the characteristics of portfolio working.

New technologies are breaking down the borderlines between work and leisure. Many now work at home with the support of their employer. Periods actually spent working are less predictable, as people are active over a more extended working week and in concentrated blocks of time.

Knowledge-based portfolio working is more likely to occur in relation to activity which:

• has a high information content
• requires minimal face-to-face communication
• relies on extended periods of concentration
• allows personal flexibility and control over the pace and timing of actual periods of work
• has clearly definable output
• involves self-contained tasks with clearly identifiable milestones
• has a modest need for access to non-electronic information or equipment
• requires modest space for storage and equipment
• values an individual's output more than the length of time he or she spends at work.

Organizational priorities, as well as developments in technology, are intensifying the demand for white collar portfolio workers, especially at the more lucrative end of the market. The most telling advantage for companies is the scope for exploiting the abilities of serial talents in quick succession.

This will enable companies constantly to recycle their stock of bright ideas through turning over a succession of short contracts with different portfolio workers. The portfolio workers will also benefit from the recyclable and marketable experience of working for a series of organizations, as well as from terms of trade that will favour the breadth of their expertise.

At its best portfolio working enables you to assert control over your lifestyle. It is no less challenging than a more traditional company-based career, in its demand for self-investment and a relentless pursuit of new opportunities for work contracts to ensure continuing employability. It therefore requires, no less than other forms of employment, a commitment to career planning and constant re-evaluation of your career strategy.

Activity for the global market: Balancing work and life priorities

It's only recently that the issue of achieving a life–work balance has become a key component of career planning and counselling. Hitherto the assumption for people at the threshold of deciding on their careers has been that most types of employment allow a reasonable balance to be maintained between the demands of working and the need to achieve a reasonable quality of life.

The growth of insecurity has brought the issue to the fore, as growing numbers have felt trapped within an inequitable psychological contract with their employers. Many employees feel frustrated at the ease with which employers can exploit the implicit threat of redundancy to make increasing demands and thereby erode personal values and commitments outside work.

It's often a particular experience or trauma that causes the employee to reassess their position *vis-à-vis* life and work. Among such events might be:

- health problems which affect motivation or work output
- threatening hierarchical relationships, for example being subject to workplace bullying or racial or sexual harassment
- burn-out
- caring responsibilities that prevent one from meeting work commitments
- demotivation as a result of lack of appreciation, demotion or failure to achieve career ambition
- a new relationship outside work, prompting a downshift in one's commitment to work.

A career strategy for the pressures of the global market requires prior reflection on the life–work balance, so that decisions aren't made in response to events over which we might feel that we have scant control. A good starting point is to identify your priorities in achieving an equilibrium between your work and your life outside work.

Choose the ten most important dimensions to your life both inside and outside work. These dimensions are aspects of work and life that you're committed to. You will find some examples below. You will probably want to add your own to the ones you choose here:

- power
- responsibility
- working with people
- income level
- status
- autonomy at work
- amount of free time
- freedom from stress
- financial security
- enjoyment of work
- fulfilment at work
- a sense of purpose
- variety of work
- opportunity to travel as part of work
- work environment that doesn't impinge on home life
- ability to lead a life outside work
- working environment that does not undermine relationships or family commitments.
-
-
-
-
-

This list makes assumptions which might not be valid in your case. For example, although I have listed "freedom from stress" as one dimension, implying that the less stress you're subject to the better, there are people who enjoy being in stressful situations and using their ingenuity to resolve them. Ask someone in the SAS.

Now let's have a look at how you rate the extent to which these dimensions are either fulfilled within your current work situation, or (for those elements relating to your life outside work) are met because the nature of your work enables you to meet your aspirations.

List the ten dimensions you have chosen (or made up yourself) in the left column of the table below. Next, for each dimension, circle one of the numbers between 1 and 10 in the adjacent columns, to represent the extent to which you feel that each dimension is being achieved given your current work situation.

A score of 1 will suggest that the dimension you consider important is absent from your life. A score of 10 indicates that you experience all that you would wish to against that dimension. For example, if the first of your dimensions is "income level", and you score it 7, then you are fairly happy with your income level, although there's room for improvement.

EXTENT OF FULFILMENT OF IMPORTANT LIFE–WORK DIMENSIONS WITHIN YOUR CURRENT WORK SITUATION

Dimension   Extent to which dimension is present in your current work situation

(1 = low 10 = high)

Dimension	1	2	3	4	5	6	7	8	9	10
•	1	2	3	4	5	6	7	8	9	10
•	1	2	3	4	5	6	7	8	9	10
•	1	2	3	4	5	6	7	8	9	10
•	1	2	3	4	5	6	7	8	9	10
•	1	2	3	4	5	6	7	8	9	10
•	1	2	3	4	5	6	7	8	9	10
•	1	2	3	4	5	6	7	8	9	10
•	1	2	3	4	5	6	7	8	9	10
•	1	2	3	4	5	6	7	8	9	10
•	1	2	3	4	5	6	7	8	9	10

Already you will see a pattern emerging, according to whether the dimensions you circled achieved high or low scores. Much will depend on how much priority you give to each of the dimensions you have identified. It might be that the majority are on the low side, indicating a number of areas where you are dissatisfied. But if there are two or three dimensions with high scores and you classify these as by far the most important to you, then you have a potentially satisfactory work situation.

What's your conclusion? Are you happy to be in work? Resigned to it? Wish you had an escape route? Your conclusions about this exercise will depend on what weighting you give to each of the dimensions, in addition to the pattern of scores you allocate.

So let's take it a stage further. Think back to what your life–work balance was like three years ago. (If you haven't been in work that long, then go back to your situation between three and six months after you first started work.) Complete the same exercise again, but in relation to the period you have identified in the past. You will need to begin by filling in the "dimension" column with your ten most important dimensions and then to complete the scoring.

EXTENT OF FULFILMENT OF IMPORTANT LIFE–WORK DIMENSIONS WITHIN YOUR PAST WORK SITUATION

Dimension	Extent to which dimension has been present in your past work situation (1 = low 10 = high)									
•	1	2	3	4	5	6	7	8	9	10
•	1	2	3	4	5	6	7	8	9	10
•	1	2	3	4	5	6	7	8	9	10
•	1	2	3	4	5	6	7	8	9	10
•	1	2	3	4	5	6	7	8	9	10
•	1	2	3	4	5	6	7	8	9	10
•	1	2	3	4	5	6	7	8	9	10
•	1	2	3	4	5	6	7	8	9	10
•	1	2	3	4	5	6	7	8	9	10
•	1	2	3	4	5	6	7	8	9	10

Now assess the extent to which your work situation has been getting better or worse over the period you have chosen. There are likely to be inconsistencies between one dimension and another. But do you detect a general trend? What does it tell you about what's happening to your life and work now, as compared with your recent past?

It will help to reflect upon some specific developments that have affected you. Think about these to assess:

• in what ways these developments have made your situation better or worse
• the extent to which they're controllable
• how important they will be in future.

Now we can complete the exercise by projecting three years into the future. What's your best guess as to how these dimensions will be scored in three years' time? You will need to take into account whether you're likely to change jobs, whether your personal or family circumstances will change, and other relevant factors specific to your life and work at the moment. You don't have to assume that you will be working for the same company as you are now, for example. But you do need to be realistic about where you might be in three years' time.

As before, start by completing the dimensions in the extreme left column, and then score each of these according to how important you believe each will be to you in three years' time.

EXTENT OF FULFILMENT OF IMPORTANT LIFE–WORK DIMENSIONS WITHIN YOUR FUTURE WORK SITUATION

Dimension Extent to which dimension is likely to be evident in your future work situation

(1 = low 10 = high)

•	1	2	3	4	5	6	7	8	9	10
•	1	2	3	4	5	6	7	8	9	10
•	1	2	3	4	5	6	7	8	9	10
•	1	2	3	4	5	6	7	8	9	10
•	1	2	3	4	5	6	7	8	9	10
•	1	2	3	4	5	6	7	8	9	10
•	1	2	3	4	5	6	7	8	9	10
•	1	2	3	4	5	6	7	8	9	10
•	1	2	3	4	5	6	7	8	9	10
•	1	2	3	4	5	6	7	8	9	10

Finally, rewrite your ten dimensions in priority order of importance, with your most important priority at number 1. Write your first set of scores again into the column headed "Present" in the grid below. Then complete the other two columns with your scores from the "Past" and "Future" exercises.

SHIFTS IN YOUR LIFE–WORK PRIORITIES

Dimension (in priority order of importance – 1 = most important)

	Past	Present	Future
1			
2			
3			
4			
5			
6			
7			
8			
9			
10			

You will now be able to see the movement in relation to your life–work priorities. What do your scores tell you?

- Are you looking forward to an idyllic future in which your work commitments and other commitments and expectations are in harmony?
- Are there danger signs which tell you that it's high time to move jobs or even change the type of career you're pursuing?
- Is your assessment fairly inconclusive, signifying a need to keep reviewing the position as you await positive developments in one direction or another?

The range of possibilities is unlimited. Whatever your conclusion at the moment, you might want to repeat the exercise every six or twelve months, to determine whether there are significant shifts in trends that you can then take into account in your career planning.

One of my witnesses was someone who found himself slipping into despair as a result of no longer being able to control his working environment or his life outside work. The stress became so intense that he fell ill and was forced to leave work. His home life deteriorated too, although the support (emotional and financial) he received from his partner saw him through the worst of his experiences.

In reliving what he went through, he told me that he could identify a point at which he had seen what was happening to him. But he had felt helpless to do anything about it because he was trapped in a specialist field and in a job that he had had for over ten years. The only strategy he could adopt was to hang on grimly and hope he could ride the storm.

This is, of course, an example of a pre-millennium career strategy. The antidote is to undertake constant self-analysis to enable you to the detect the signs of impending difficulties and to take action before it happens. This self-analysis can give rise to such action as:

- investment in updating skills
- developing new skills as a fall-back
- creating and extending networks of potential contractors for the skills and expertise you have
- toe dipping in alternative work activity (e.g. writing professionally or dealing in a product which you have some expertise in)
- preparation for self-employment
- commitment to changing jobs and companies often enough to keep alive your career prospects outside your current firm
- building up sufficient savings to be able to invest in your own training, professional development or business
- being prepared to downshift, knowing the consequences including the effect of having a lower income
- taking out an income protection policy
- investing in your own mobility, either within the UK or beyond
- negotiating with your current company a career contract that enables you to develop your skills and experience to prepare yourself for the possibility of life outside the company.

This is not an exhaustive list of possibilities. Others will occur to you which relate specifically to your own circumstances. Write down a list of strategies you could pursue if your work situation were to become unbearable. This is not to suggest that you should pursue any of them now. But it's important to have some idea of what you might do if things got tough. Doing your thinking beforehand reduces the potential for making bad career choices when you're under pressure or suffering from stress.

What strategies could you adopt if you needed to change the direction of your career. Write down as many as you could realistically pursue.

ALTERNATIVE CAREER STRATEGIES
(CONTINGENCY PLANNING)

-
-
-
-
-
-

You might never have to put your strategy into effect. But even if you don't, the fact that you have one reduces enormously the worry, insecurity and potential stress of having to change direction because of a difficult work environment.

Thinking for the global market

Let's summarize some key components to a strategy that tackles uncertainty and enables you to maximize your ability to ensure that the demands of career and life outside work can be kept in balance.

1 Don't be mesmerized by the glare of insecurity

Data on the average length of stay in a job shows much less turnover than many commentators imply. There's often a feeling of security associated with carrying on in your present organization, whatever the prospects in reality. Many are tempted as a result to stay in their current job, rather than take the risk of moving to another organization.

So if you're staying, do so for the best of reasons – as a conscious career investment or a way of maintaining your quality of life. Log what those benefits will be. If you're minded to move on, work out the balance sheet of advantages and disadvantages compared to your current position, and take your decision on the basis of the tangible evidence that you compile.

2 Invest in your own flexibility, wherever you are

The confident executive is one who isn't going to burn him- or herself into a state of excessive stress. He or she will realize that, although short bursts of all-consuming energy are inevitable, there are limits to the time that any individual can work.

The level of confidence will be determined by the individual's employability. Even when you're working very hard, if you're not simultaneously developing your skills, then you're harming your long-term prospects.

Keep looking forward; ask yourself what you're going to do next, how you will acquire the skills and competences to do it, and how you can use your current organization to get you to that point.

3 Look for a new niche in your current organization

There's a place for imagination in every company. Make a habit of analysing your own organization to work out where the gaps are and if you could fill one or more of them. It's the newly created posts that will attract attention in an organization. They will be the ones most amenable to development in directions which interest their holders.

The very exercise of identifying the gaps will enable you to focus on where opportunities might arise in other organizations, and to prepare yourself accordingly. One recurring theme of the interviews I conducted for this book was the frequency with which individuals had spotted an area for development in their organization, colonized it and used it as a springboard for further career progression.

4 Look out constantly for new opportunities

Be assertive. If you don't look out for opportunities to develop from within your current working situation, it's all too easy to see the years rolling by and to realize too late that you're suspended helplessly on the end of someone else's line.

Graham Whitehead of British Telecommunications illustrates, from his own experience, the need to be proactive in looking for new career opportunities.

> What I've done throughout my career is to drive it myself. I've done everything from making lasers to packaging integrated circuits to throwing cables off the back of cable ships, to running production lines, to what I'm currently doing which is basically acting as a marketing manager for research.

What you need is the sheer get up and go to leap into the dark. When the door opens, it isn't going to be open for long. But you've still got to leap. The big problem is there might not be a light on in the room you're leaping into. You've only got it on trust there's a floor. But get in there.

When a door slams in your face another one opens. But the one slamming in your face is right in front of you. The one opening is down the corridor. Look for it. Gone is the time when you can just sit here, do your job well and get promoted. That's dead in most major companies. It's the people who get on and do it, who are the people who are going to win in the future.

Don't think of yourself as developing your skills only on those occasions when you participate in formal training. You can do it every day on the job. The judgement you need to make is in relation to the nature of the opportunities that arise and how to exploit them in a way that enhances your value to the company. Offer solutions to problems. Compile your own achievement file for use as part of your portfolio.

5 Don't let anything eye-catching on your portfolio get dated without having first replaced it with something as good

Jane Kingsley, managing director with Russell Reynolds Associates, the recruitment consultancy, explains that the first thing she looks for on a CV is what the person has been doing most recently, and particularly whether that experience relates to what she's recruiting for.

You can't afford to make a feature of something that might have been state of the art two or three years ago, but is now dated. Hence the need constantly to get access to prestige projects to give yourself the appeal you need to make the transfer to the next stage of your career.

6 Look to work for a company that makes its career investment offer explicit

Negotiating a career investment package at or before point of entry is a shot in the dark as you won't know the strength of the competition. You will be in a better position to negotiate a training or experience investment after six or twelve months in the company, when they will have had sufficient opportunity to assess your contribution. By then you will also have benchmarked yourself against others in your field at an equivalent point in their career development.

7 Work out your negotiating strategy and have it ready for when you are appointed

We have seen how negotiation between the bigger companies and their prospective employees is becoming more intricate and sophisticated, as a result of global developments in the employment market. If your job application is successful, you need to think beyond narrow reward packages. Seek commitment from your employer to invest in you. But demonstrate, in addition, the benefit that such an investment will have for your employer.

8 Exploit opportunities to network

An individual's value derives not from their place in the organization's hierarchy, but from the respect their colleagues have for them. That in turn is based on their performance record. Talented new entrants to the labour market now use networking as a standard way of gaining their first contract. They then use that first job as a launchpad from which to make further contacts.

Work on making contacts outside your company and step up your visibility. You're more likely to be taken on by somebody else, if they know you and trust you.

Creating Opportunity from the Global Market

From iron track to global network

About 150 years ago labourers toiled all over Britain blasting tunnels, building up embankments, digging cuttings and laying down iron tracks. Very few understood the significance of what they were doing.

The railway revolution generated immense self-confidence. There seemed no obstacle too great, no challenge too daunting, that it couldn't be overcome by the combination of ingenuity, technical expertise, manpower (as it was, then), finance and an indomitable British spirit. Building the Manchester–Liverpool railway across the infamous Chat Moss bog, the grand design of St Pancras Station – these and other civil engineering and architectural triumphs symbolized a nation that believed itself to be the greatest in the world.

By 1850 when a national network of railways had been created, the railway navvies (as they were called) had generated the seeds of a revolution which transformed the way work was organized, how people spent their leisure time, the way they thought about their physical horizons and the country they lived in, even how they used the English language. These iron tracks shaped the peoples of Britain into a single nation.

The construction of the railways completed the economic system created by the Industrial Revolution – cheap labour, plentiful raw materials and mass distribution, all combining to create wealth.

The economic system that has served the developed world for the last century and a half is giving way to one based on the processing of information and knowledge. Roads are being dug up in the UK and elsewhere to lay down optical fibres. Doubtless

many of those doing this work don't appreciate the unprecedented nature of the telecommunications revolution that they're
introducing.

These fibres will carry cosmic tracts of information instantly
across great distances. That information will extend beyond the
printed word. Sound. Pictures. Moving images. Data that can be
manipulated from thousands of miles away. A technology that will
scatter brainwork to all parts of the globe.

In addition to processing and transferring data, the information
and communication revolution will enable industrial activity to
be controlled from thousands of miles away. An operative working
with a video link and remote control facility from Bogota can
manage a robotic assembly line in a Bradford factory as effectively
(and more cheaply) than one based in the room next door.
Specialist surgeons using sensitive remote control technology can
perform delicate operations on patients thousands of miles away.

Researchers are experimenting with systems that exploit data
recorders implanted inside equipment, to enable repair work to
be carried out via the Internet. The data recorder transmits data
on operating conditions to the manufacturer. The supplier can
then use the data either to send a replacement, or to input a
command downline to get the equipment working again.

Apart from eliminating the need to send back faulty equipment,
the cheapness and universal accessibility of such a service illustrates the global nature of the economy and the labour market
which services it.

In contrast to the railway revolution, there are no great monu-
ments to show for all this breathtaking technology. Nor is there
an accompanying feeling of national pride or optimism. On the
contrary, it is a source of growing anxiety, even though we have
only begun to appreciate its effects. The feature of this revolution
that causes most dismay is its cocktail of accelerating change,
global scale and bewildering unpredictability.

However, it is the very pace and capriciousness of change that
generates opportunities for those who are prepared to fathom its
properties and exert control. Politicians all over the world have
detected a new source of electoral capital in the insecurity
unleashed by the global economy. In this chapter we identify
sources of global change, and corresponding textures of behaviour, attitudes, skills and experience which can be woven to create
the strength and versatility to meet the challenges of the global
market.

The forces of globalization

Information and communication technology alone have not created the global economy. There are other forces driving populations which are separated by vast distances to become at the same time both interdependent and subject to the dynamics of competition on a global scale. These forces are:

• the progressive removal of trade barriers
• growing fluidity in the movement of finance
• the proliferation of multinational companies
• the increase in international technology transfer
• accelerated movement of people across national boundaries
• improved education levels in developing countries.

The world economy is becoming increasingly integrated, as companies routinely make global choices about locations for investment and sourcing for production. Markets for products and services are global, as are flows of investment funds and profits.

With production organized on an international scale, firms are able to establish a presence in major foreign markets, gain efficiencies and customize products for local markets. The requisition of inputs and supporting services from around the world enables firms to exploit the specialization of many countries and minimize costs. Cross-border alliances and joint ventures with other companies are another key feature of the global economy, giving companies the benefits of combined assets, shared costs and the ability to enter new markets.

Capital markets and national economies interact on a global scale. Large-scale movements of employees have become common, especially within multinational companies. New technology-based applications ricochet around the global economy as international industry-research networks are established to generate and propel innovation throughout the economic system.

Movement between levels within class structures is also accelerating. Frank Vogl and James Sinclair, authors of *Boom: Visions and Insights for Creating Wealth in the 21st Century*, predict that an expansion lasting some thirty years will invigorate the world economy. They argue that emerging markets will spur hundreds of millions of people to rise from poverty to form new middle classes. Supplying their customer demands and building the necessary infrastructures, especially in parts of Asia, Latin America and Africa, will create huge opportunities for western business.

The increase in the supply of labour in developing countries is another significant element in globalization. The growing availability of education has created a new workforce, albeit a large proportion with relatively low skills, but far from unskilled.

In 1960, the average length of time spent in schooling in developing countries was 2.4 years. By 1986, this had more than doubled to 5.3 years. There is still some way to go, but an increasing proportion of workers in developing countries have the skills necessary for manufacturing employment. This encourages outsourcing and relocation of manufacturing capacity by western firms to developing countries.

At the micro end of the economic scale too, the separation of knowledge from organization and place enables people to use knowledge wherever they happen to be located without having to go the places where it is collated, processed and stored. Knowledge businesses will multiply as a consequence, driven by a new breed of knowledge entrepreneurs working either for organizations or adding to the numbers of the self-employed.

For those who are prepared for the scale and velocity of change in the global market, a lifetime of fulfilling, rewarding and stimulating work is both realistic and achievable. We need to analyse the major concomitants of global economic change as they shape the labour market, in order to identify how to generate sufficient bandwidth of opportunity to animate that ambition.

The features of economic change which impact on individual positioning in the global labour market can be summarized as:

- the erosion of national boundaries
- recruitment systems that operate on a global scale
- the impact of imported talent
- global labour pricing
- the emergence of a global class system.

We now examine the implications of these phenomena for those seeking a permanent niche in the global labour market.

The erosion of national boundaries

One part of our identity which is hardwired into our minds is the country we belong to. Almost every form we fill in asks for our nationality. Our loyalties in top-class sport are expressed in terms of national allegiance. Bookshop shelves are stacked with titles satirizing the alleged amorous excesses of the French, revelling in the past monarchical glories of the English or celebrating the foibles of Australians.

While the bond between nostalgia and nationality is likely to remain strong for some decades yet, the information revolution is busily dissolving the demarcations represented by national frontiers. Communication technology is turning the world into a single, information-driven economy.

This development is reinforced by the fragmentation of political power and the corresponding emergence of regions of economic interest. The resolution of the political conflicts which have divided the economic world for most of the twentieth century, including the breakdown of communism, the end of the cold war and the collapse of apartheid, has had a significant impact on international openness.

In 1978 one-third of the global workforce lived in centrally planned economies. Another third lived in countries which were linked only tenuously to international trade, because of high protection barriers. Most of the world's population now lives in countries that are highly integrated into the world economy, or in countries like China, India and the states of the former USSR, rapidly becoming so. These countries make up nearly half of the global workforce. It is estimated that by the turn of the century, fewer than 10 per cent of all the world's workers will be cut off from the economic mainstream.

Economic affinities rooted in ethnicity and diaspora are beginning to supplant nation states as the key units of economic vitality. Supranational political structures such as the European Union are creating new magnets for political power through funding mechanisms which reward cross-national regional alliances.

The population of northern Japan might have greater interest in fishing deals made with eastern Russia than in regulations issued from Tokyo. Wales and Scotland could end up participating in more powerful economic partnerships with New York, Hong Kong or Paris, than with London.

The west has not yet recognized the power of the "bamboo" network of fifty-seven million overseas Chinese. The peoples of the European Atlantic seaboard, from rain-sodden Galway to the sun-baked Algarve, are linked in an association based on common economic interest and on cultural affinities rooted in their Celtic past.

Differences in economic well-being will become wider within a single country – as, for example, some parts of China are now twenty times richer than others. Even within the UK the gap between the wealthiest and the poorest regions is widening, with the south east of England enjoying a gross domestic product some 43 per cent higher than that of northern Ireland.

When a local out-of-town supermarket opens it can have a devastating effect on local traders. We will see similar rapid inflows and outflows of wealth in the global market. Many local communities worldwide are set to become impoverished as their wealth is attracted to distant shareholders.

Rosabeth Moss Kanter's *World Class: Thriving Locally in the Global Economy* recognizes that local communities are threatened by global ownership. Local markets and employment can be destroyed by decisions taken thousands of miles away.

In his book *The World in 2020 – Power, Culture and Prosperity*, Hamish McRae suggests that the power of governments will decline as international markets and multinational companies become stronger. He argues that it will be pointless to look to governments to create jobs or provide better social services. Governments will be powerless to maintain national prosperity. The marketplace will ensure that resources flow to those who best meet world demand, whoever is in government.

The multinational corporations account not only for a growing proportion of cross-border trade, but they are also a major source of new investment in technology, jobs and skills. Since the mid-1970s, the multinationals have grown more quickly than the world economy. In addition, the old national "champions", such as Ford, IBM, ICI and Mercedes Benz, have tried to break free from their national roots, creating a global auction for investment, technology and jobs.

As capital movements have been eased, the mass production of standardized goods and services has shifted in large measure to countries, regions or communities with low wage costs, light labour market regulation, weak trade unions and benign fiscal conditions such as tax holidays and subsidized rents. Forty per cent of jobs created by British multinationals were located overseas in the 1980s.

The global competition for inward investment has the characteristics of a Dutch auction. Corporate investors play off nations, communities and workers in a bid to increase their profit margins. This results in bidding spirals in a downward direction, which impoverish local communities and workers by forcing concessions on wage levels, rents, and taxes in exchange for investment in local jobs.

There are trends which are taking the edge off national self-determination, such as an accelerating cultural change which is dissolving distinctions between different national markets. Once countries reach a certain level of prosperity, patterns of consumer demand become similar.

This is reinforced by mass advertising. Often the reason for a consumer preference for imported goods, especially among high income groups, is the desire for novelty and variety. This becomes a self-perpetuating trend as the scope increases for economies of scale to be secured from supplying a similar range of products to markets in a number of countries.

Although McRae and other writers in the same vein have deposited their doomy relics, their case is exaggerated. Governments throughout the developed world are addressing the economic, social and political implications of the information age and the global market. One example is the European Union's aim to counter the power of the financial markets by progressing towards a unified currency, with all the fiscal disciplines that that brings.

In addition, more enterprising individuals are coolly assessing the implications of the global economy, so that they can make the most of the opportunities that arise. As long as government-sponsored planning falls short of making the best sense out of these trends (a fairly sound prognosis, one would have thought), there will be plenty of business in risk management, with a mission to minimize the potential dislocation which is endemic to the global market.

No country is a risk-free zone in the global economy. The ability of any national government to underwrite the economic security of its citizens is limited. But this does not imply that the global work strategist has to adopt a pinball machine approach to deciding where to base himself or herself, or to become subject to global concussion fatigue engendered by oscillating from one country to another in search of a secure niche.

While the economic erosion of national sovereignty might engender despair among devotees of "land of hope and glory" nostalgia, for the global work strategist it should be seen as one of a series of value-free trends which have to be factored into their calculations.

Thinking for the global market

The nation state is waning as the cardinal global economic unit. Here are some ways in which you can deal with the consequences of this development by taking advantage of the opportunities of the global market.

- Get connected to relevant global data communication networks.
- Seek work contracts abroad.
- Extend your awareness of political, economic and social developments in a handful of countries to which you might accord "preferred destination" status.
- Develop a network of international contacts.
- Adopt a lifestyle that doesn't tie you down to a particular location for a long period of time.
- Gain experience of living in foreign countries.

Activity for the global market: Thinking beyond national boundaries

Now think about your own situation and reflect on how to shape your own strategy for taking advantage of opportunities in the global market. Three examples are set out below. Add in three of your own.

SHAPING A STRATEGY FOR THE GLOBAL MARKET

- List the countries that my current company does business with. Arrange an appointment with the relevant sales manager and ask for her views on the prospects for career development in those countries, related to my particular expertise. Ask her for the names of other contacts and for useful sources of information.
- Assess my freedom of movement, e.g. in terms of family, partner, friendship and social commitments, property, etc., both now and over the next three years. Is the situation likely to stay the same? Can I reduce my commitments and so increase my mobility? Set out how this might be achieved over the next three years.
- Extend my social and leisure activities in directions which will bring me into contact with people from a wider range of national and cultural backgrounds.
-
-
-

Global recruitment

The growing fashion among large multinational companies to adopt globally consistent recruitment disciplines is further cause to escape from the traditional CV mindset. The Association of Graduate Recruiters has detected a globalization of graduate recruitment materials, especially among the multinationals.

Investment bank SCB Warburg has standardized its recruitment procedures for graduates applying for jobs anywhere in the world, putting them all through the same process. Regardless of where they're located, all candidates are selected according to the same criteria. Warburg's offices across forty-two countries previously recruited using different selection criteria and assessment tools.

British-American Tobacco has also adopted an international approach to its recruitment. British-American Tobacco's first global recruitment campaign in 1996 aimed to take on at least 300 graduates from fifty countries. They join the company as trainee managers on a two-year development programme. Michelle Healy, graduate recruitment manager of British-American Tobacco, extols the advantages of a recruitment campaign which applies consistent standards throughout the world.

More far-reaching possibilities are illustrated by Reed Personnel Services' launch of the UK's first video interviewing network. Candidates sit in front of a computer terminal with a videoconferencing camera mounted on top of the monitor. On the screen in front of them they see the video image of the person interviewing them.

Derek Beal, deputy chairman of Reed, sympathizes with interviewees who are technophobic. But he stresses the benefits in terms of saving employers' and candidates' time and money. The company has plans to make the service available in half of its 200 UK offices. Whitehead Selection, a search and selection company, has been carrying out video interviews with a view to shortening timescales and speeding up shortlisting.

It's important for candidates to be natural in remote interviews, and not to be put off by the starkness of the studio environment. The camera and the screen are often slightly apart, so discipline yourself to look at the camera. Don't glance back at the monitor when you're speaking, or you will give the interviewer the impression that you're watching a Grand Slam tennis final.

A new industry is growing up in the wake of this development, viz. coaching job seekers in techniques which cater for the video interview. High-flying jobs usually specify a requirement for communication skills. This requirement will soon extend to media and remote communication skills.

Dow Chemical, which employs 8500 people in several European countries including the UK, manages the whole of its European staff as a single workforce. This means measuring productivity, recording personal development, and matching skills in one region to opportunities in another. The company has rationalized its personnel systems, after incompatible procedures had been introduced to different parts of the business. Dow's financial systems have also been integrated.

Another company, Logica, has undertaken a major initiative in global personnel systems, which is summarized in the next case study.

Global work group selection: Logica

Logica is a software house with its corporate headquarters in the UK. The company extends its globalization disciplines to the selection of its own staff for particular assignments. It thereby provides a model for the globalized company of the future. Logica's organizational shape and operating systems are likely to be replicated by companies whose workforce in large measure consists of highly educated staff who travel from one metropolis to another as part of their working routine.

The company was conscious of the need to build up their relationships with global players such as Barclays, Reuters and Ford, which demand the same level of service whatever the location.

Logica offices all over the world have computer screens hanging from the ceilings of social areas, to keep staff informed of company performance, share price, key projects and vacancies around the world. Because reward and opportunity are strictly tied to performance, Logica consultants are encouraged to continue to find work in project teams in different parts of the world, matching their particular skills to whatever projects are going on.

The company has 5000 staff in eighteen countries. They're all part of the same pool of resources. That means that individual employees have to move between project teams and countries as a way of enhancing career development, and managers need to utilize the expertise of the whole organization, rather than what they happen to find in their particular business unit.

Logica has also introduced an international staff movement policy to ease the relocation of staff across countries. They have up to the minute records of staff training and experience. These show which skills each individual has, so that they can be matched to particular projects. Staff need to keep their CVs up to date, written to the company's format.

The Logica culture requires staff to sell themselves to customers. Each employee is responsible for keeping his or her own credentials up to scratch recorded in CV format and then used by the individual and Logica as a skills marketing tool. It's recognized that an individual's rewards and market value are based on skills and capability but increasingly international experience is a key factor in enhancing career development.

More companies operating across national frontiers are set to follow the Logica example by revising their personnel and reward systems to make them consistent and co-ordinated across the various countries where they're active. National boundaries are less relevant to Logica now than they were even five years ago.

One practical issue for anyone intent upon creating opportunities from the global market is to draw up a CV, résumé or portfolio to fit requirements that can vary significantly from company to company and country to country. We will look at this issue in more detail in chapter 7. The next case study shows how what might appear to be just a technical matter can pose a challenge to one's beliefs and values.

Beyond belief: Alex Rink

Alex Rink, now studying for an MBA at the INSEAD European business school, has pursued a management career in motor manufacture and logistics. Canadian by birth, he encountered difficulties the first time he looked for a job in Portugal.

> I was very naive. I expected things to run the same way as they do in Canada. I expected there wouldn't be any significant changes, not to something as simple as writing a résumé.
>
> In North America we have a certain way of writing CVs. You were trained in how to write your résumé, how to market yourself and so on. When I went to Portugal, I took these skills and made up my résumé. I

showed it to some people and they suggested all kinds of changes.

And I couldn't understand how the changes would help me. They were suggesting putting in all kinds of information that in North America would be illegal, or if not illegal, would be grounds for discrimination.

In Portugal a CV is an incredibly elaborate document. On the personal information section, apart from your name and your permanent address you put in all kinds of things like the name of your mother, when you were born, whether you're single or married.

They were telling me to put this in my CV and I said, "There's no way I'm putting this in my CV." And this highlighted my difficulty in adapting because I simply couldn't believe that this was the way that they wanted CVs. The honest truth of it is that the people who were looking at my CV were uncomfortable with it.

It was maybe too flashy or too showy. This bit about using different fonts. In Portugal a lot of people just typewrite their résumés and it's often a three- or four-page document, and you go on and on about what you've done. Because it had been so ingrained in me in Canada, I felt this was going backwards. But anyway in the end I did it.

As CVs and their successors eventually become more standard-ized globally, we can expect multinationals to make their own assessments of national education, training and qualification systems and the skill levels which they denote. Not only will we be in competition with one another (as we already are now) within our national education system. We will also find ourselves prioritized for potential employment according to informal league tables each company draws up for itself of education systems in different parts of the world.

Given the relatively lacklustre performance of the UK's educa-tion and training system other than at degree level, many will find themselves in danger of being outclassed not necessarily by the performance of other nationals, but by the superior global status of their qualifications.

Activity for the global market: Preparing for global recruitment practices

Global recruitment practices will have a growing impact on career thinking. You will need to reflect on, and revise, your global career strategy in the light of these developments. Re-engineering your portfolio and presentation repertoires will become a regular routine, and will include new disciplines.

Consider how you might respond to the following strategies in order to prepare the ground for the challenge of global recruitment practices:

- continuous updating of skills
- conforming to company templates
- defining your unique selling points
- stressing your global versatility
- acquiring qualifications (and wider recognition of achievement) with an international currency (e.g. International Baccalauréat, Duke of Edinburgh's Award)
- becoming comfortable with remote communication for the purposes of selection
- positioning yourself for work projects calculated to add new dimensions to your experience.

Are there practical ways in which you could take forward these strategies, and others you devise yourself? Log them below. Two examples are provided.

PREPARING FOR THE ONSET OF GLOBAL RECRUITMENT PRACTICES

- Research three individual multinational companies and three UK-based companies in my area of work to see what qualifications they are demanding at different skill levels. Keep a log of the extent to which these requirements change over the next year.
- Arrange an appointment with my personnel/training manager, and ask her to review my skills in comparison both with what I have discovered through the previous component of this activity, and with those of new recruits to the company over the past year. Work out an action plan and ask her to comment on it, and then to support me in further training/professional development.

- •
- •
- •

The tide of imported talent

The limitations of focusing on your home country when assessing your career expectations are thrown into sharp relief when you consider the market value of (non-UK) European and Asian high flyers to leading multinational companies.

Mainland Europeans are better placed in terms of their global communication skills in foreign languages to take jobs offered by UK firms, than are their UK counterparts who aspire to be taken on by mainland European companies. English is the foreign language that most mainland Europeans learn in school and college. It's the choice of 65 per cent of those in the fifteen to twenty-four age group.

In addition, increasing numbers of mainland European pupils are learning more languages. Two-thirds claim to be able to speak a second foreign language. Forty years ago the figure was one in three. Denmark now expects every school leaver to be bilingual (at least). Every European Union member state except the UK has made learning a foreign language compulsory in primary school.

10 per cent of scientists involved in scientific research and development centres across Europe are foreign nationals. In the Netherlands and Switzerland, this figure goes as high as 30 per cent. Companies give as reasons for recruiting foreign nationals not only specialist skills, but also the desire to build an international culture in the organization. Recruits have come not only from other countries in Europe, but also the USA, China, Japan and eastern Europe.

Even more intensive competition arises from Asians who complete their education in Europe. Multinational companies are scrambling to employ Asians from European universities. They have identified these young people as a growing pool of talent to be tapped. Standard Chartered, international bankers, recently ran a programme to recruit nationals from fifteen Asian and African countries who were studying at universities in the UK, the USA and the Netherlands.

Shell, British-American Tobacco and Marks and Spencer (now operating in Hong Kong and Singapore) have also scoured Europe for Asian graduates. There are currently more than 100 000 students from Asia studying in Europe, and their numbers are growing every year.

It's easy to see why this group has been targeted as twenty-first century high flyers. To secure a place at a European university, students from Asia must be talented intellectually in addition to being multilingual. Kitson Smith of EAP, the European business school, has also noticed that Asian graduates are marketing themselves more assertively. He has detected that students from Asia, instead of appearing more modest than their European counterparts as in the past, are now feeling more confident, especially as the economies in their home region have become so successful.

The shortage of western managers who have either the language skills or the appreciation of Asian cultures gives Asian graduates from European universities a clear advantage in the competition for the most rewarding jobs.

The small number of Europeans who have the commitment to learn Asian languages and get to grips with Asian cultures, as well as developing their professional expertise, will be much better placed to secure attractive contracts than their European competitors who do not make the necessary investment in these skills.

As yet there is scant evidence of corresponding interest among Asian companies to employ European graduates. Many dismiss Europeans because of their image as inhabitants of a squabbling continent of fading former colonial powers whose workers are well-fed leisure junkies unwilling to accept change.

Even western multinationals operating in Asia are raising the commitment they expect. How many westerners, for example, would be willing to accept Procter and Gamble's terms for becoming a marketing manager in India, i.e. living for twelve months in an Indian community in order to internalize the lifestyle of the people who make up the potential market?

Thinking for the global market

The defeatist response to the international impact of labour market trends would be to take refuge in a mindless xenophobia. That would not only be a waste of effort; it also misses the point. Managerial talent, whatever its national origins, will add to the sum of global wealth if it is directed effectively. The size of the global pool of contract opportunities isn't fixed.

One needs to be aware of the nature of the competition and to respond intelligently. That doesn't mean that you will have to learn five Asian languages in order to secure a lifetime of work.

It might mean concentrating on one Pacific Rim language and developing an appreciation of the different values and working cultures of other national groups, to enable you to negotiate effectively, to market more successfully or to work more creatively in a multicultural team. It could well make it easier for you to develop the global network of contacts that is an essential component of planning for the challenge of the global market.

The growth of imported talent indicates the determination of leading companies to enlist the services of the most gifted people available to achieve their goals. At this level of employment, there are no fixed formulas for success. But awareness of the growing intensity of competition that this phenomenon denotes can lead to new directions in self-investment, including:

- fostering of multicultural understanding and sensitivity in a business context
- openness to fixed-term periods of experience abroad
- acquisition of niche skills which will add value through rarity
- foreign language acquisition
- keeping an eye to the possibilities for anticipating and exploiting the problems, e.g. miscommunication and cultural incompatibility, created by these very developments.

Global labour pricing

This is not the place for an analysis of the determinants of the price of labour. Currency levels, tax regimes, welfare systems, employment legislation, wage levels are all factors that affect global positioning of countries in the labour market.

High labour costs in Europe have created strong incentives for capital to be substituted for domestic labour, or for capital to be used abroad to escape high labour costs. Favourable wage costs in east Asia especially have attracted western technology and capital on a huge scale. European wages are three to four times higher than those in Asia. European Union investment in Asia is now worth more than £2 billion per year.

The International Labour Organization, in its report on world employment in 1995, estimated that 30 per cent of the world's workforce are underemployed. This is the highest figure since the Great Depression of the 1930s. Another report, from the Organization for Economic Co-operation and Development, predicts that by 2000 Europe's unemployment rate will not fall below 9 per cent. The report adds that about two-thirds of the thirty-three million people looking for jobs in the industrialized world are European.

When eastern Europe was opened up to competition from the west, factories closed down. Hundreds of thousands were thrown out of work. Communities were destroyed. These former communist bloc countries were only catching up with those regions in western Europe and North America whose previously dominant manufacturing centres had collapsed, in the face of successful competition from other countries.

Further examples are shipbuilding and car manufacturing which have vanished from Tyneside and Detroit respectively. They have left urban wastelands. Towns previously dominated by single companies are being replaced by global production lines, where work is subcontracted to the lowest bidder. These global chains spread far and deep, even to rural parts of south-east Asia, where homeworkers are making parts for windscreen wipers that end up in the cars driven in Detroit.

The whole of the developed world is now facing this challenge. Competition is no longer restricted to the trader from down the road, or a narrow group of companies operating in the same country or even continent. The competition now comes from the best in the world who, because of global communication, might as well be living on the doorstep. Distance is no bar to penetrating new markets.

Already India is showing unprecedented success in global markets, even though for its 860 million people there are only seven million telephone lines, virtually all of them concentrated in a few large cities. China, too, is developing its competitiveness faster than anyone imagined, with the additional Asian advantage of cheap labour.

Africa is likely to remain the exception in terms of the participation of the majority of its population in the global economy. Other than South Africa and some north African countries with connectivity to the European economies, most African countries rank as non-viable entities in the global economy because of:

- the fragility of their economies
- the low price and limited uses of their primary commodities
- the narrowness of their markets
- the unpredictability of their politics
- the inefficiency of their bureaucracies
- the low skill levels of their workforce
- the primitiveness of their telecommunications infrastructure
- their inability to attract significant inward investment.

In Europe political leaders are involved in endless discussions about the impact of the introduction of a single European currency. There is little doubt that, in the early years, a single currency will result in greater unemployment throughout Europe, given the requirement for tight controls on public spending, inflation and interest rates. A recent study by the National Institute for Economic and Social Research predicts that, if all the member states were to achieve the entry requirements, one and a half million jobs would be lost.

In the past, the UK has used devaluation of its currency to remain competitive in the face of better performance by stronger economies in Europe and worldwide. This is unlikely to be an option once the euro is jingling in the tills of the European mainland, whether or not the UK joins the currency union. Weaker regions will lose this mechanism to renew their competitiveness, leading to increased bankruptcies and relocations to areas with lower wage costs or more skilled labour. The weaker countries will suffer greater loss of employment, as the eastern part of Germany found when it achieved monetary union with west Germany.

There will, though, be plenty of opportunities for the alert global strategist. A single currency will make the purchase of property across national boundaries much easier. It will set a trend for a long-term relocation southwards, where property prices are much lower. In the information society, you can place your virtual office in your home as effectively in Seville as in Southampton. And if your costs are lower in Seville, you will be more competitive. People will be moving southwards not primarily for the sun, but in pursuit of their business imperatives.

The USA and Europe have been affected by the transfer of high-level computing and software jobs to India and to other less developed economies, where skill levels are high and wages low. Technology is available particularly through satellite communication, to allow interactive contact with clients. When SwissAir decided to use computer links to transfer its booking function to India, the work was done more cheaply, but as quickly as had previously been the case in Switzerland.

Such transfers of business can benefit the developed economies too. KITE, a company based at Kinawley, County Fermanagh, Northern Ireland, employs fourteen people who process data remotely for organizations all over the world. It attracts contract work, particularly from the USA. From the point of view of its US customers, KITE offers the added benefit of completing the data processing overnight.

There will continue to be opportunities in Europe, despite the predictions that Europe is in trouble because it is overpaid and overburdened with welfare costs. In recent years inward investment into the UK has exceeded £8 billion annually, creating hundreds of thousands of jobs. The UK commands 40 per cent of all Japanese and US inward investment into the European Union.

A recent survey of large American companies suggests that a majority expect to expand their business in Europe over the next five years, with massive and lasting investment. The survey, conducted by Deloitte Touche Tohmatsu International, concludes that while in the US the media tend to focus on Asia and Latin America, a large number of American companies will concentrate on Europe, which they perceive as an up and coming market.

The USA concentrates two and a half times more of its foreign investment in Europe than in Latin America, and three times more than in Asia. Predictions are that this European lead will be maintained. Whilst other continents are favoured for their cheaper workforces, and Asia also is strong on government subsidies, Europe is still attractive because of the broadly comparable standards in terms of purchasing power and lifestyles.

In addition other similarities in product and service standards mean that the cost of developing a new product or service can be spread over a wider market: Europe has a population of 370 million, compared with the USA's 260 million. Infrastructure, in particular telecommunications and terrestrial transportation, is also identified as a significant plus point, together with deregulation.

There is no room for complacency, though. Economic competitiveness will intensify as an increasing proportion of the world's population gains access to the global telecommunications infrastructure. At the moment half the world's population lives more than two hours' travel time from the nearest telephone. This bars them from the information and data networks that telecommunications provide.

But more countries will invest in relatively low-cost satellite-based systems to produce advanced, broadband information infrastructures in areas where it would not be economically feasible to install optic fibres. Satellites have a wide area of coverage which can make them cost effective. As more countries get connected to global telecommunications facilities, labour markets will become more volatile and the price of labour will become more market sensitive.

Thinking for the global market

The instability of global wage economics reinforces the need to develop long-term career strategies which are sufficiently malleable to enable the career strategist to switch to new options quickly. That points to the need for:

- constant intelligence gathering on the state of the segment you are engaged in
- continual self-investment to keep a range of options live
- a willingness to trade immediate financial reward for longer-term investments in your own skills and expertise
- investment in broader skills and knowledge in preference to over-specialization.

The global class system

In *Beyond Certainty*, Charles Handy describes three types of workers in the global labour market. The first group he refers to as career fundamentalists: high-flying managers who are uncompromising in their dedication to the organization, and are prepared to sacrifice their personal lives into the bargain. Working all hours of day and night, many burnt out by middle age, they're generously paid, highly talented core workers for the organization, rewarded for as long as they continue to maximize profitability.

The second group are the lesser-skilled operatives. They can be clerks, traditional secretaries, cleaners, cooks, sales people – a whole range of occupations which do not require initiative, exceptional communication skills, or competences that take longer than a few hundred hours to develop.

Handy argues that these are the people at most risk in the global market. Their contribution becomes increasingly marginal to the organization they work for. The organization doesn't reward their loyalty, as it can undercut them by hiring another worker or company to do the work. These people are on the threshold of becoming the new underclass, and the older they get the less chance they have of reorienting their skills and attitudes to take them further away from a fringe stake in their society and economy.

The third and newest element, according to Handy, is those who by choice or circumstance are not permanent employees attached to a single organization. They invest in their own skills, market themselves continually, take on contracts from several organizations at the same time, and map out their own individual career patterns and progression.

Having developed an expertise, product, skill or service, they put together a portfolio that demonstrates their intellectual assets, and they then go out in search of customers. These "portfolio people" are particularly suited to the new type of economic activity increasingly referred to as knowledge working. Handy has predicted that society will be divided according to the access one has to information, rather than by social or financial status.

It's questionable whether Handy is simply dressing up a well-established group of workers in parvenu clothing. For "portfolio person", read the self-employed. Many involved in the building trade would be able to point to their handiwork in reroofing, pebble dashing, patio laying or drainage clearing, in Handy's terms. And self-employed entrepreneurs with portfolios of leather goods or a string of successful contracts in herding sheep go back to the Bronze Age.

Handy's analysis is simplistic in its characterization of three broad categories of workers. But if one looks in more depth at the effects of changes in the organization of work on society at large, one can detect significant developments in labour stratification which will impact upon global career strategies.

The concentration of financial power in global cities and the dispersal of manufacturing have had far reaching consequences. Manufacturing produced lots of middle income jobs in the 1950s and 1960s, leading to a significant growth in the numbers within the middle class. But the new jobs in the financial sector today divide almost equally between those at the top (executives and analysts), and those at the bottom (clerks and administrators).

This has created two-tone divisions in cities such as New York, Tokyo, Frankfurt and London. Rents rocket where the new executive class live; expensive restaurants and leisure outlets open. New centres of inner city high life are created.

Around Canary Wharf in London, for example, shops and services are springing up which cater exclusively for the needs of the affluent classes who work there. Rosabeth Moss Kanter has detected, in her *World Class: Thriving Locally in the Global Economy*, the emergence of a new cosmopolitan class who meet at airport shopping malls worldwide.

But even the well-off in these cities are aware that they have to struggle hard to keep their position. The telecommunications infrastructure, the availability of international airports and quality of life, are now the factors which determine whether the vast financial sector stays in London or leaves town for Zurich, Frankfurt or New York.

The knowledge society is accelerating these trends. In his book *Cyber Business Mindsets for a Wired Age*, Christopher Barnatt explores the world of electronic information as one of the new frontiers in employment. He points out that, across the world, millions are already communicating by computer and most clerical activities have been computerized.

In Barnatt's view, more management functions will be performed by software agencies with minimal human input. He suggests that a new information-handling élite will emerge and, at the same time, a technically illiterate underclass will also be created.

Some observers have noticed the growth of virtual companies – organizations without a single physical presence. They predict a rapid increase in businesses that are effectively networks of people with particular skills. A virtual company is one which has organization – it's just that you can't see it. It doesn't have an office. You get to it on the telephone or via a fax or modem.

Typical is the virtual company, Red Spider. This is an international network of media planners founded in 1994 in Scotland. It has individual employees based all over the world. It has no office. Its managing director, Charlie Robertson, describes it as a series of collaborative, global thinking networks. The company generates good ideas; and Robertson accepts that these are as likely to emerge in the bathtub as in the office. So why have an office?

A related development is that we will see a huge transformation of multinationals into global holding enterprises, which will apply a core of common systems, e.g. with respect to accountancy practice, but then leave them to operate autonomously. The communication between the federation of these entities will be minimal, though they will be accountable separately to the holding organization. This could create a new type of global career which prizes achievement within a new breed of virtual satellite entities.

Whether the global business world will be dominated by chameleon-like companies of one form or another has been the subject of fierce debate. It's easy to exaggerate the potential effects of the information revolution and the information superhighway on the way we organize ourselves.

One hypothesis is that the information revolution will lead to the collapse of hierarchies – political, economic and social. The theory is that, because information is power and everyone will have access to information, those who have traditionally been at the top of hierarchies controlling information will have the ground cut from under their feet. Modern communication technology – telephones, fax machines, copiers, modems and the networked personal computer – have broken this stranglehold on information.

While it is true that information technology has encouraged decentralization in organizations, it remains to be seen whether it will generate myriads of small, networked virtual businesses, ruthlessly stripping out everything but the core business and doing all their work through contracts and networks, so that other firms will supply services and raw materials, distribution and assembly facilities.

The age of the large, hierarchical organization is not yet over. It will continue to provide plenty of opportunities for work. It's too easy to generalize from the computer sector to the rest of industry and commerce.

Certainly an industry like information technology, the main characteristic of which is the breathtaking speed at which the technology itself is developing, does reward small and flexible firms. But in many other areas of economic life, from building aeroplanes to fabricating silicone wafers, there is still a need for ever-increasing amounts of capital, technology, well-educated people and huge organizations to co-ordinate the complexity of effort required.

Another feature of globalization is the growing disparity in income levels both within and between countries. In 1996 the United Nations Human Development Report stated that the total wealth of the world's 358 billionaires was equal to the combined incomes of the poorest 45 per cent of the whole world population, i.e. 2.3 billion people. The person at the top of the wealth hyperleague is Bill Gates, founder of Microsoft, whose estimated personal wealth of $18 billion is enough to enable him to buy half a dozen poor countries.

Those on the way up in the Forbes World League Table are the digerati of the information revolution, together with entrepreneurs thrown up by the east Asian miracle economies.

At the same time, in seventy of the world's countries, people are on average poorer than they were in 1980. In forty-three countries they are poorer than they were in 1970. Inequality has grown between countries, but within them as well.

Average income per person in the UK is £11 000, but the bottom 20 per cent earn only £2500, according to the United Nations report.

The digital billionaires are making fortunes faster than anyone else in history. In previous generations, billionaires would be ambitious businessmen (there weren't many women), who derived their wealth from building products like cars which involved an assembly line and the creation of tens of thousands of jobs round the world. Now, it's down to software.

Bill Gates and Paul Allen, both in the Forbes top ten, have gained their position this way. Netscape, founded by James Clarke, wasn't heard of in 1994, but soared to more than $3 billion on the stock market after its flotation. Netscape makes one of the most popular browsers for the Internet, enabling users to surf between computers all over the world to search through a network of world databases for information and find it in a matter of seconds. Netscape's software is installed on an estimated thirty million computers worldwide.

The information revolution has the capacity to raise educational standards all over the world, thereby contributing to a less unequal society. Instead, it is producing a new breed of millionaires, who are widening inequalities with products that divide the world into info-rich and info-poor countries.

Increasing polarization in income is far more pronounced in the USA and UK than in any other Organization for Economic Co-operation and Development country. In Germany there has actually been a decline in income differentials.

Significantly too, the increased dispersion of income is not associated with those countries, such as Japan and Sweden, which are
leaders in applying new technology. It is more evident in the USA
and UK, which have fallen behind in this respect.

Thus increased dispersion of income is not necessarily the result
of the changing cognitive and skill demands of work. Raising skill
levels does not necessarily result in a commensurate increase in
income, through the operation of the global labour market. Other
factors are more important; for example in the UK the decline
in unionization in the 1980s accounts, according to some
researchers, for 20 per cent of the increase in wage inequality.
Employment deregulation has exacerbated the trend.

Thinking for the global market

So where does that leave the global career strategist? Let's put
together our analysis earlier in this chapter on the dissolution of
national boundaries and labour market pricing, with this – admittedly complex and uncertain – movement towards extreme labour
market stratification, which involves much greater differentiation
than was evident a generation ago between those at the top of
the income scale and those lower down.

The result is a strengthening of bonds between people of
different nationalities who identify with a particular line of profes-
sionalism or vocation. It used to be only high flyers among the
medieval and Renaissance clergy, through the Catholic Church
and especially its papal headquarters, who enjoyed a power base
and source of support through a global network.

Now it's almost everyone with a specialism that requires years
to develop: architects, surgeons, actors, publishers, property
dealers, etc. And what's interesting is that, for the most successful,
international communities are being established, based not on
physical proximity (with some notable exceptions such as the
celluloid entertainment fraternity in Hollywood), but on global
networks which provide moral as well as professional support.

There's nothing wrong in this of course. For many, the prospect
of extremes of nationalism being replaced by forms of association
reminiscent of the more principled functions of the medieval
guilds is a source of satisfaction and relief.

What it does for the global strategist is to provide ready-made
networks to tap into, for sources of professional support and

renewal. But it can also lead to complacency, if it is relied upon completely and uncritically. The medieval guilds collapsed under their attempts to exert monopoly power over craft specialisms. The global market is too fluid to allow organizations devoted to restrictive market manipulation to prosper.

Activity for the global market: Making contact

In this chapter you have contemplated some challenging issues. For some the invitation to assess their state of preparation for phenomena like the erosion of national boundaries and global recruitment might have engendered a degree of perplexity.

The issues are disconcerting because they need thought and analysis, leading to action. The associated activities you have already addressed in this chapter aren't quick fixes. They represent an investment of effort intended to provide a foundation for a lifetime career strategy.

In the final activity of this chapter, we want to take stock of where you are now in your preparation and how your experience and attitudes shape up for the potential of a lifetime of activity in the global market.

Activity for the global market: Frontiers of understanding

Complete the responses below by ticking one box for each statement.

1   If I were to face the prospect of living abroad in an English-speaking country, I would feel:

A   ☐ very confident.

B   ☐ fairly confident.

C   ☐ apprehensive, but willing to give it a try.

D   ☐ unable to cope.

2   When travelling abroad:

A   ☐ I welcome the opportunity to make new friends from that country and to keep in contact with them.

B ☐ I don't look out for opportunities to make contact with people from the country, but if I find I get on well with someone, I'm happy to keep up the contact when I get back to the UK.

C ☐ I pursue contacts only with British people.

D ☐ I keep myself to myself.

3 If I needed to apply for a job abroad, I would:

A ☐ have a clear plan of the steps I would take.

B ☐ have some idea of how to go about it.

C ☐ not know what to do, but be prepared to research it.

D ☐ neither know how to, nor have any inclination to start.

4 If at work I were asked to deal (in English) with foreign visitors from a different cultural background, I would:

A ☐ feel very confident about my ability to relate to them effectively.

B ☐ feel fairly confident about my ability to relate to them effectively.

C ☐ feel apprehensive about my ability to relate to them effectively, but be willing to give it a try.

D ☐ suggest that someone else should be asked instead.

5 In a mixed ethnic group I feel:

A ☐ confident and natural.

B ☐ apprehensive, but willing to find common ground.

C ☐ uptight and defensive.

D ☐ out of my depth.

6 If I were to face the prospect of living abroad in a country where the dominant culture is "western", I would feel:

A ☐ very confident.

B ☐ fairly confident.

C ☐ apprehensive, but willing to give it a try.

D ☐ unable to cope.

7 In a mixed social group (i.e. with people from different social backgrounds), I feel:

A ☐ confident and natural.

B ☐ apprehensive, but willing to find common ground.

C ☐ uptight and defensive.

D ☐ out of my depth.

8　When I am the only person of my gender in a social or professional gathering, I feel:

A　☐ confident and natural.

B　☐ self-conscious, but able to converse freely.

C　☐ uneasy and awkward.

D　☐ embarrassed and struggling to find my words.

9　If I wanted to seek a work placement abroad from my employer, I would:

A　☐ feel very confident about going on such a work placement.

B　☐ feel fairly confident about going on such a work placement.

C　☐ feel apprehensive about going on such a work placement, but be willing to give it a try.

D　☐ not pursue it for lack of confidence.

10　My friendships:

A　☐ extend mainly to people who don't speak English.

B　☐ extend mainly to people who speak English, but not as their first language.

C　☐ extend to some people who don't speak English as their first language.

D　☐ are restricted to people who speak English only.

11　When I'm abroad in a non-English speaking country:

A　☐ I make an attempt to use the local language, however poorly I speak it.

B　☐ I use a combination of English and sign language.

C　☐ I use English only.

D　☐ I try not to talk to anyone.

12　If my company has a foreign delegation visiting it:

A　☐ I offer to help with hospitality, including accommodation if appropriate.

B　☐ I do my best to meet them at least once.

C　☐ I make no effort to meet them, but am happy to socialize if I come across them.

D　☐ I try to avoid them.

13　If I were to face the prospect of living abroad in a non-English-speaking country, I would feel:

A　☐ very confident.

B　☐ fairly confident.

C　☐ apprehensive, but willing to give it a try.

D ☐ unable to cope.

14 In terms of cultural heritages other than my own, e.g. Kashmiri, Buddhist, Traveller or Celtic:

A ☐ I value them all and like to find out more about them.

B ☐ I respect them, though I wouldn't go out of my way to find out more about them.

C ☐ I tolerate them, but from a strictly neutral point of view.

D ☐ I believe that people in the UK should adopt the "British" way of life.

15 If my company offered me the option of several weeks' work abroad in the coming year, I would:

A ☐ welcome it with enthusiasm.

B ☐ be willing to go, but want to find out more.

C ☐ be willing to go, as long as it didn't interfere with my other plans.

D ☐ suggest they ask someone else.

16 If I were to face the prospect of living abroad in a country where the dominant culture is non-western, I would feel:

A ☐ very confident.

B ☐ fairly confident.

C ☐ apprehensive, but willing to give it a try.

D ☐ unable to cope.

17 If I were part of a work team with people from different nationalities but who all spoke English, I would:

A ☐ feel confident and excited about the prospect of a new experience.

B ☐ expect difficulties, but do my bit to get people working together.

C ☐ expect difficulties, but not go out of my way to resolve them.

D ☐ carry on doing things the way I like to, multinational team or no multinational team.

18 One's line manager can be crucial to one's performance and well-being at work . . .

A ☐ but I don't mind what their gender or cultural background is, as I can work professionally with anyone.

B ☐ so I would prefer to work with a line manager of the same gender, though I wouldn't have any problems about someone with a different cultural background.

B ☐ so I would prefer to work with a line manager of the same cultural background, though I wouldn't have any problems in relation to difference of gender.

D ☐ so I would prefer to work with a line manager who has both the same gender and cultural background as me.

19 If I wanted to do voluntary work abroad, I would:

A ☐ have a clear plan of the steps I would take.

B ☐ have some idea of how to go about it.

C ☐ not know what to do, but be prepared to research it.

D ☐ neither know how to, nor have any inclination to start.

20 If my company were to send me abroad on an assignment for twelve months, I believe I would:

A ☐ acclimatize easily and enjoy the experience.

B ☐ expect difficulties, but try my best to make a success of it.

C ☐ get downhearted because I was away from home.

D ☐ try to get the assignment shortened or terminated.

Count up the number of A responses you gave, the number of Bs and so on. Enter the totals below. Then work out your total score on the basis of:

- four points for each A response
- three points for each B response
- two points for each C response
- one point for each D response.

SUMMARY OF YOUR RESPONSES

Score

A responses   × 4

B responses   × 3

C responses   × 2

D responses   × 1

Total score:

Feedback

A score of **sixty or more** shows you highly accomplished in the communication and interpersonal skills that can do so much to bring about success in a business environment which involves contact with people of different social and cultural backgrounds.

You're also very self-confident, a problem solver able to take responsibility, to see opportunities and exploit them to your advantage. As business becomes increasingly focused beyond national boundaries, your outward-going nature will be seen as an asset to any organization.

A result **between forty and sixty** gives you a promising base to work from. You are tentative in some respects, and perhaps can't quite see yourself dealing with assurance with all the challenges, especially the unforeseen ones, that come your way. However, your attitudes show a willingness to learn and to reciprocate. It is perhaps the depth of experience that you lack. So it's important for you to build on your strengths, to capitalize on opportunities that come your way, and to take the occasional risk.

A total of **less than forty** indicates an anxiety or possibly hostility towards the unfamiliar. You aren't at all comfortable with the direction in which the global economy is taking us. While this might allow you sufficient opportunity to secure your income in the short to medium term, unless you're in the twilight of your career, then your attitudes will create barriers to your career progression and personal development. I imagine that the very fact you have put yourself through this exercise represents some recognition on your part that there is a potential problem here and that you want to do something about it. If this does reflect your view, then you deserve credit for your willingness to re-examine your views and values. As with many issues associated with interpersonal relations, one's acknowledgement that there is an issue to be addressed is the first, and most important, step in working towards a solution.

You will almost certainly have found helpful the other activities you have come across so far. And there are more to tackle in the remainder of this book. You will find, though, that you make most progress in developing a positive attitude towards the challenges of the global market, if you seek, and seek to enjoy, contact with people from different backgrounds. It's the ability to communicate with and relate to people from all parts of the world that will become increasingly valued in business and social milieux in the decades to come.

Thinking for the global market

The earlier explorations in this chapter do raise long-term areas for development that really can't be delivered overnight. They are explored further in the next three chapters of this book.

From this chapter you will have picked up the following key points.

- You don't need to relocate outside the UK to make the most of the opportunities of the global market.
- Global communication networks are good enough to enable anyone to run an international business with minimal resources.
- Networking internationally is more important than ever.
- Experience of living and working abroad is invaluable.
- Training in the use of video technologies will pay dividends.
- Although knowledge of foreign languages isn't critical, it brings success so much closer.
- You need to keep up with developments in your area of expertise, and especially what's going on in other countries.
- Keep reviewing the information and achievements that you log for inclusion in your personal portfolio, in the light of changing expectations of global recruiters.
- Work on your attitudes and behaviours where these betray less than complete confidence in diverse social situations.

Cerebral Fibres: Making Good the Education Deficit

The purpose of this chapter is not to provide a polemic on the failings of the UK system of education and training. Many complain of the UK's position in the so-called international education league. But the pecking order of national education and qualification systems is as subjective as the reputations associated with individual universities and local schools.

This chapter addresses the needs of the individual who wants to develop their skills, knowledge, understanding and attitudes by exploiting education and training opportunities, and by extending their bandwidth of achievement beyond what the UK system provides.

This in turn requires an understanding of the more conspicuous source of myopia evident in the UK education system, i.e. its failure to address convincingly the implications of the knowledge economy. What are the features of this economy and how will it impact upon the way we invest in ourselves as miners of data, hewers of information and shapers of knowledge?

Trading in knowledge

Over the past 100 years, gross domestic product worldwide has increased by a factor of twenty. But the global economy weighs about the same now as it did then. It is the weightlessness of the economy that is critical to our understanding of the profound changes that are hurtling through the industrialized economies and which require new configurations for our human resource capital.

We tend to think of economic value being represented in physical substance: a house, a car, a motorway or a satellite. But this interpretation is becoming less tenable as the economy dematerializes.

Dematerialization is the tendency for the value produced in our economies to be embedded in computer memory or biological memory, rather than in material things. For most of this century the industries which created most value have been the "heavy industries" combined with manufacturing: shipbuilding, car production, machine tools and, more recently, domestic "brown" goods.

The electronics revolution, miniaturization and the use of new materials has enabled the same or increased value to be embodied in less weight. Cars, for example, are smaller and weigh less, but they carry greater sophistication in terms of their on-board audio, communication and navigational equipment. Weight loss has been accompanied by increase in value.

Paradoxically, this compression in the nature and value of products is a consequence of developments in one segment of the service industries. The traditional service sector comprises community and personal services: health care, education, welfare support, cleaning, hair care and so on. The bulk of these are in the public sector and they aren't significant in the context of the dematerialized economy.

The service activity that is paramount here resides in hi-tech areas such as DNA sequencing and software development. It also includes specialist financial services and mass entertainment. This segment relies on information and communication technology. Its economic value far outstrips that of the traditional services.

This sector is expanding exponentially because of Moore's law. Gordon Moore is chairman of Intel and he calculated that the computing power of the microchip doubles roughly every eighteen months. Not only does this cause prices to tumble; it also makes computing power ubiquitously available.

Twenty years ago in the USA there was one computer in use for every 1000 people. By the year 2000 there will be more than one between two. The corresponding figures for the world are one computer per 15 000 people twenty years ago and one computer for eleven people by the turn of the century.

Thus the important development in the major industrial economies is not, as many have argued, the switch from manufacturing to services per se, or even from low to high technology.

It is more in the movement away from producing machine tools or freight tankers, to creating software and DNA sequences. These illustrate the essence of the dematerialized economy.

Danny Quah, author of *The Invisible Hand and the Weightless Economy*, argues that dematerialized economies are different, not only because ideas are more important and can be communicated more easily, but especially because of what he describes as the infinite "expansibility" of products. The fact that I'm using a software programme to word process this book doesn't stop anyone else anywhere in the world from using the same software. Many other products have the same characteristic: other software, any broadcast content, books, articles, films, management tools, anything on CD, CD-ROM and so on. In the USA, the dematerialized industries are bigger than defence and car manufacture.

So we can see how globalizaton at the end of the twentieth century is different from the globalization which occurred about a hundred years ago, and which arose from the growth of trade and overseas investment. The current phenomenon is not increasing the exchange of goods and services; rather it's multiplying their reproduction. There are no limits. Search engines, a Spielberg movie, a process for designing yourself a customized car, this book – all are infinitely replicable.

A second important feature of dematerialized industries is their relatively low initial capital costs: you don't need to invest in a vast petroleum refinery or an assembly plant. One person, a computer and a modem is all you need to start trading.

A third characteristic of dematerialized products is their "network externalities". That means the extent to which they're used by people. If sufficient numbers use a product like the search engine Yahoo, then the demand for it will grow simply because everybody else is using it. It doesn't have to be the best system. It just needs to be the one that a sufficient critical mass of people are using.

A significant consequence is the encouragement to widen income differentials in the developed economies. This is because these activities enable people with the most marketable skills to sell their output to a wider global market. People with less developed skills are left competing against others with similar skills from lower wage economies.

Dematerialized products are based on the application of knowledge. The implication of the knowledge-based economy is that your potential wealth is in your head. Or more likely, as the complexity of knowledge-based products increases, it's located in the combined heads of groups of people working together on the right concept at the right time.

Global knowledge wars

One consequence of the knowledge-based economy combined with the significance of effective teamwork is that wealth creation depends upon nations and companies being able to exploit the skills, knowledge and insights of workers in ways which cannot be delivered through Fordist, mass production techniques.

Enterprises now depend on quality as much as the price of goods and services. They need to find new sources of productivity and investment. Such value-added enterprises are most commonly found in companies offering customized goods and services, e.g. in microelectronics, financial services, consultancy, telecommunications, marketing, advertising, biotechnology and the media.

The UK, in common with other western countries, has been looking to its social institutions and human resources to meet the global challenges it faces. It has learned, particularly from Japan and the Asian tiger economies, that the human side of enterprise is the critical factor in winning competitive advantage. Economic prosperity depends on raising the quality and productivity of human capital.

The new raw materials of international commerce are generated from knowledge, learning, information and technical competence. Hence the drive of governments in the developed economies to upgrade the quality of their education and training systems.

The diminished power of nation states to control the economic environment has forced them to compete in global knowledge wars. The increasing importance attached to education in the global economy reflects the fact that nations are increasingly including the quality of their human resources in their definitions of national wealth.

The international qualifications catwalk

As the drive to develop human resource capital intensifies, governments all over the world are conducting campaigns to market the qualities of their national workforces in order to attract inward investment.

This has created growing interest in international comparisons between education systems and their outputs. Comparative international data on educational achievement is notoriously difficult to interpret. A marginal adjustment to a statistical assumption can cause a country's apparent performance to soar or a league place to plummet.

Even so, many comparative studies show that the UK's education system demands less of young people at the age of sixteen in relation to technology, foreign languages, mathematics and science than do the national education systems of Germany, Japan and other countries.

The World Economic Forum ranks the UK as twenty-fourth in the world for the quality of its people skills. The government's Skills Audit Report recently concluded that staff recruited from the UK to forty multinational companies needed more training than those hired from France, Germany, Japan, the USA and Singapore.

A recent survey by Coopers & Lybrand found that only 30 per cent of employers saw the availability of skilled labour from within the UK as a source of their own competitive advantage. This compared with higher expectations of their respective workforces among French (45 per cent) and German (55 per cent) employers.

Eryl McNally has noticed within her European Parliament constituency of Milton Keynes and Bedfordshire that people in international firms don't rate UK qualifications below degree level very highly. They don't believe there's less intelligence or less creativity in this country – far from it. But they don't think that our A levels produce a student as resourceful as do, say, the *Abitur* or the *Baccalauréat*.

The Confederation of British Industry's report, *Realising the Vision: A Skills Passport*, describes the best outputs of the UK education system as world class, but concludes overall that "the UK fares badly in terms of the achievements of its school leavers, its expectations of the education system, and in the value it puts on learning".

Many employers have expressed concern that there has been a drop in standards at degree level, but George Turnbull, director of public relations at the Associated Examining Board, dismisses the argument that the expansion of higher education in the UK has resulted in falling standards: "Thirty-eight people climbed

Mount Everest in a single day recently. Before 1953 nobody had climbed it. Does that mean it's got any smaller? It's the same mountain. So who's arguing that our mountaineers must be getting worse because lots more of them are climbing Everest?"

Many of my expert witnesses were concerned that, despite the absence of conclusive evidence, many multinational companies and large firms with a UK footprint saw the UK education and qualification systems as deficient, especially at the higher achievement levels.

Jonathan Bratt, global account director at A.C. Nielsen, specialists in marketing research, predicts recruitment being opened up to foreign nationals as a consequence. He himself receives correspondence in better English from first-language French, German and Italian speakers than from UK nationals. He expects this pressure to increase if UK academic standards are perceived to be declining. Other witnesses also concluded that there would be a greater temptation to recruit from overseas for jobs within the UK, although they had not seen tangible evidence of this yet.

There is a danger in the longer term that the pressures of the knowledge economy will result in a devaluation of UK-based qualifications in much the same way as sterling has reduced in value since Britain came off the Gold Standard in 1931.

It's essential to make contingency plans for the eventuality of suddenly finding yourself classified, because of the national origin of your qualifications, in a junior world division of talent. We will come back to this issue in the context of higher education later in this chapter.

New team working dimensions

The concept of human resource capital extends beyond the sum of individual talent available to a company or country, to the added value that can be generated through effective deployment in teams. The culture of individualism which is evident in the UK and other western societies tends to work against full realization of the potential of team work. This cultural norm marks out western societies from Asian cultures, which stress family and community values to a much greater degree.

Although there is a general understanding of the importance of team work to a company, its significance to the success of an organization is often underrated even within the organization itself. As Francis Fukuyama argues in his book *Trust: The Social Virtues and the Creation of Prosperity*, people who can work together for common purposes in groups and organizations have a potentially unlimited ability to create wealth.

Fukuyama explains that if people who work together in an enterprise trust one another because they're all operating to a common set of ethical norms, then the costs of doing business reduce. This is one reason why Japanese business practices have been so successful: Japan enjoys a culture where there is a high degree of trust exercised through mutual responsibility.

The opposite occurs where people don't experience mutual trust, but rather co-operate only under a system of formal rules which have to be negotiated and enforced. This legal or quasi-legal apparatus serves as a substitute for trust and entails what economists call transactional costs, which within companies can include the opportunity costs associated with the invocation of grievance procedures and submission of complaints to industrial tribunals.

Thinking for the global market

Against this background it is evident how the UK education and training system provides inadequate exposure to the disciplines and rewards of working in teams. For example, our assessment and qualification systems are almost entirely founded upon individual achievement.

This is not intended as criticism of the UK education system. All education systems have their flaws. Arguably Asian systems which emphasize the pre-eminence of the social unit above the individual create for those economies complementary issues of excessive deference and reverse ageism which can also incur costs to companies and communities. It is important, though, to identify those elements within the education system one has been through which constitute potential blindspots or weaknesses that need to be adjusted by individual action.

That individual action needs to address those elements in our education and training system which leave us inadequately prepared for the demands of the knowledge economy. We shall now examine the provision made by schools, universities and employers, applying our analysis of the economic imperatives of the global market in order to assess where individual initiative can make up the deficit.

Learning by rote

Developments in information and communication technology, changes in the organization of work, the infinite possibilities for the replication of knowledge and the direction of the global economy are between them creating the need for flexible, adaptable individuals who can invest their abilities in a succession of teams to add value to their product or service.

By contrast the compulsory education system in the UK is wedded to Taylorite principles of production:

• The emphasis is on passive receipt of knowledge rather than active learning.
• Students are combined into homogeneous cohorts by age, and often by gender and ability.
• They are put through courses of standard lengths.
• Their working days are regimented and predictable.
• They are subjected to a monolithic curriculum.
• The focus of learning is the school building, rather than the vast sources of knowledge available from remote sources.
• Their achievements are benchmarked against national norms in defined and restricted areas of learning and experience.
• Achievement is assessed formally on the basis of outcomes produced by the individual, rather than by teams or groups.
• Assessment tasks are designed for closed contexts, to the detriment of experience associated with devising appropriate definitions of problems.

One understands the need to organize formal education in a standardized way. But such a framework neglects competences essential for long-term security in the global economy, such as:

• research skills to access information remotely
• disciplines associated with team work which is both face-to-face and at a distance
• organization of work within flexible time frames
• understanding that asking the right questions can be more important than coming up with the right answers.

These issues struck a chord with several of my expert witnesses. Christopher Bissell, head of department of telematics at the Open University, has observed the extent to which graduates see themselves as solvers, rather than definers, of problems: "It's far more difficult to look at a complex situation and set it as a problem which is to be solved, than to take a problem which somebody gives you and says, 'Right. Solve it.' Once you have identified the problem, that might be really all that you need to do."

Eryl McNally MEP criticizes the mechanistic principles behind the system of National Vocational Qualifications, which take the problem-solving orthodoxy to the extreme of not even having to understand how what you have done actually contributed to the solution of the problem. McNally recalls: "An electrical engineer told me that as long as the trainees had done certain things, it wouldn't matter if they thought that little fairies carried the electricity round the house, because they had actually wired the plug and done whatever else they needed to." A system that endorses someone's ability to do something without testing the theory behind it is no use to anyone, she concludes.

A visit I made to a multinational chemicals company with its headquarters in Germany elicited a similar perception, but from the standpoint of a training system which has resolved the issue of the need for underpinning knowledge and understanding. The head of training took me to a control centre and explained:

> In the sixties and seventies, we just told people what to do with the switches that controlled the dials. Beyond that they didn't need to know what was happening. Today we tell them what chemical compounds they're making and how they react together. Our technicians understand the effects of what they're doing with those controls.
>
> That means they can make intelligent suggestions themselves on what the problems are and how to solve them. They can act on their own initiative when they need to, and that cuts down our supervision costs. Above all they can take action early if something is going wrong. Twenty years ago they would have just sat around in blissful ignorance while a whole production run was being spoiled.

Thinking for the global market

Bissell's and McNally's observations indicate some of the areas for development which individuals will need to pursue in order to make up for the inevitable gaps in their formal education.

Flexibility is clearly an essential asset in an environment where business success depends upon the ability to apply knowledge which is increasingly ephemeral, from within teams which will constantly break up and re-form.

In that context we can't afford the luxury of making a single strategic decision about career direction and self-investment. Tony Webb, director of education for the Confederation of British Industry, characterizes career paths as akin to crazy paving, and suggests that this requires a frame of mind which enables us to bring about changes in direction by reviewing our skills, expertise, organizational base and career strategy.

Masters classes: Is one degree enough?

Record numbers are participating in higher education in the UK and it's expected that one in three young people will be attending the university sector by 2000. The number of people gaining their first degrees has virtually doubled since 1979. The UK's rate of graduation is one of the highest in Europe. By 2001 the number of graduates in the workforce is projected to be well over three million, which is twice the number in 1981.

It used to be that graduates could expect to slot into high-status jobs. But with universities and higher education institutions in almost every city and town, the supply of graduates exceeds demand. Graduate status is no longer considered a mark of distinction. These days the graduate is the kid next door. Lots are going into very ordinary jobs.

Since the redesignation of polytechnics as universities, a debate has been raging about whether a single degree is enough and whether the choice of college or university in which you study has as great an impact on your employability as the type of course you choose.

Graham Whitehead, advanced concepts manager at British Telecommunications, has noticed employers responding by going back and asking for people's A level grades, as a way of filtering. Instead of asking which university you went to, they want to know how good your qualifications were to get you there in the first place. Eryl McNally MEP speculates that the increasing numbers of graduates might take employers in the opposite direction, i.e. assessing ability on the basis of higher degrees, or identifying an unofficial hierarchy of universities.

A report from Industrial Relations Services, *Graduate Recruitment and Sponsorship* (1995), found that more employers considered the new universities (i.e. the former polytechnics) produce lower-calibre graduates. The employers questioned also felt that the teaching in these establishments was no more relevant to the concerns of business than that of the traditional universities.

It may be that employers are looking for wider skills and achievements to confirm what the degree itself is intended to convey about an individual's abilities. Attitudes such as those revealed by Industrial Relations Services indicate that although degrees are an important requirement for employability, they aren't enough on their own. But they also imply that collecting a folio of further degrees isn't necessarily the answer either.

What is essential is to find ways to make your abilities distinctive. Graham Whitehead treats a degree as no more than the applicant's ticket to be interviewed as part of British Telecommunications' selection process. After that, they have to show commitment and flair:

> Personally I don't care where they've been or what their degree is. I'm looking at how quickly and how deeply they think, how they make judgements. I'm not too interested in knowledge. Experience certainly. Somebody who's shown they can get up and go and do something, rather than just sit in a study bedroom and churn their way through examinations.

Anglian Water uses a more systematic scheme for scoring initial applicants against the core competences they're looking for. These are:

- flexibility
- initiative
- team working
- customer service
- getting on with others.

Beyond these, they look for other indicators of distinctiveness. Typically applicants are asked to name the three most important activities they have initiated or what they're proud of. David Taylor, employment development manager at Anglian Water, comments: "At one level someone will actually say they've saved someone's life. For someone else it'll be they got up in the morning and that's about the sum total."

Anglian Water use their scoring system to get an initial feel for an applicant. Their weightings also acknowledge the importance of foreign languages. This is also used as an indicator that if someone is fluent in two languages in addition to English, they're also likely to have developed some cross-cultural awareness.

Thinking for the global market

Even the evidence that's supportive of the quality of UK higher education suggests that having a good degree only gets you to the starting block in career terms. You still need to find ways to show you're different or even unique. You don't necessarily have to be better than everyone else. You need enough that's distinct about you to make people think you could make a unique contribution to their business or organization.

It might be something as simple, though challenging, as showing leadership through participation in the Duke of Edinburgh's Award Scheme or Operation Raleigh. Alternatively it could be a one-off event that doesn't gain formal accreditation.

Other possibilities include:

- taking a leadership role in a university society
- organizing a high profile event as part of a team
- a work experience project with measurable outcomes
- participation in a project with an industrial sponsor
- completing a voluntary work project abroad.

There's no set formula. Although the demand for team players is growing, there will also be opportunities for diffident types with compensating talents, for example in the arts world. Inventors and designers can be oddballs who add value exclusively through the strength of their ideas.

Trainer spotting: Whose interests do training courses serve?

Executives trust their employers to show commitment to their career development, according to the careers counselling consultancy, GHN. But this confidence is naive and misplaced. In the age of the portable career, it's up to the individual to map out a career strategy. Even those employers who show genuine commitment to career investment cannot make decisions on behalf of their employees in the way that companies used to do in the age of the job for life.

The extent of indifference among employers is demonstrated by their collusion with the de-skilling associated with 70 000 young people trapped in low-status training schemes in the UK. Furthermore the European Information Service reported in 1996 that training-into-work schemes, both in the UK and elsewhere in the European Union, fail to take account of new areas of work which are developing as a result of the application of new technology.

There is also evidence that people who have invested in developing high-order skills are not used appropriately in their organizations. Hilary Metcalf, researcher with the Policy Studies Institute, argues in *Future Skill Demand and Supply* that many employers do not use the highly developed skills their employees possess.

The UK labour force is highly mobile, with employees ready to move from one company to another. In this environment many employers are reluctant to invest in training and development. Some employers resist providing effective training as vigorously as they agitate for a high-skills workforce: they see it as someone else's responsibility to pay for the training. But the consensus breaks down when employers are invited to define what those skills are. What emerges is a cocktail of conflicting responses.

Where employers do fund or provide training, much of it is short-term and context specific. The Department for Education and Employment admits that employed people can't rely on their employers to provide them with the full range of skills they need to keep up their employability.

The Investors in People standard has prompted some progress in establishing a vehicle through which organizations can assess their training and development against a standard of good practice. It is, though, a scheme that stresses the value of the training to the organization rather than to the individual.

Some companies improve their training and development profile as a result of the demands of competitiveness. David Taylor of Anglian Water recalls how his company changed after privatization. It converted itself from an organization dominated by engineers and chemists undertaking technical processes, to one which promoted understanding of the human side of the business: "We realized that you have to deal with customers and therefore it's about having a wider range of softer skills."

Subsequently Anglian Water moved into the international field and then thought of their business as dividing into three segments:

> The middle chunk we're pretty good at. If you want something built, something to be run, then we've got the expertise. Where we weren't so good was winning the business – bidding and competing. And then at the other end, there was transferring the skills and getting out and working with people. These posed new challenges for us and we have worked hard to develop the necessary skills.

Thinking for the global market

There is a continuum of views among employers about career development. Some do actual damage to the longer-term prospects even of their most loyal employees. Others see their responsibilities as extending beyond achieving the immediate business objectives of the company, to helping employees through training, development and other support mechanisms.

It's essential, then, to allow as much for employer cynicism about career development as for potential enthusiasm:

- Find out as much as you can about the organization you intend to work for.
- Define your negotiating position in terms of the long-term investments you want to secure for yourself, before you agree to a contract.
- Don't assume that training programmes that are good for the company are necessarily good for you.
- Make your own assessment of employee development activities offered by your employer, against the yardstick of your own career strategy.
- Guard against work experience and training programmes which narrow your longer-term career options.

Investing in career futures: Generic skills or specialization?

Our argument so far in this chapter is that people who want to maximize their career options have to make up a deficit evident from:

- a system for the compulsory years of education, the monolithic values of which leave insufficiently developed skills and experience, which are essential to survival in the global economy
- higher education provision which appears to deliver too much of a good thing, so that the individual has to add to their profile in order to convince prospective employers of the distinctive nature of their capacity to add value to the organization
- employer attitudes to on-the-job training and career development which can range from wholehearted and focused support to negligent indifference.

This places the onus on each of us to structure our own career planning on the basis of a broad scan of the environment in which we intend to operate. In the remainder of this chapter, and in the two subsequent chapters, we will focus on the key elements of this broad scan approach to developing a career strategy for the global market.

One of the debates associated with career planning is the extent to which one should try to anticipate the needs of the labour market and go for an area which might be in short supply. We looked at this issue in chapter 1 and concluded that, although it was useful to study trends in various occupational sectors, there wasn't a simple correlation between expanding and declining areas of work and long-term employability prospects in those areas.

Developing career strategies is not a matter of picking winners among industrial sectors or occupational areas. Hence the concern of Dick Whitcutt, director of Industry in Education, over the specialization implicit in the General National Vocational Qualifications framework:

> Employers would like to see GNVQs being broad skills based, divided only into very rough clumps of occupations. The danger arises when the interest groups muscle in and say, "Yes, but accountancy is different from book-keeping. So we want one in this and one in that."

We have seen how, just as the technology of mass production led to the assembly line and its management hierarchy, so information and communication technology is creating organizations which value generic skills as opposed to excessive specialization. It's more effective for a single individual to take an order, arrange delivery and send out a bill, than to establish separate departments to perform those functions. The customer also benefits from more personal service.

So companies need employees who have a broad education and who are versatile, rather than ones who have been trained exclusively to perform specific tasks. These broadly skilled people can command higher salaries because of their scarcity value. At the same time those with outdated, context-specific skills, are subject to falling remuneration. The single skills part of the workforce accounts for a disproportionate section of unemployable people at the bottom of the labour market.

The implication is that well-rounded employees are more valuable than those emerging with single track vocational training qualifications which concentrate on a narrow range of skills that could swiftly become outdated.

Another strategy gives you the best of both the generic skills and the specialization options. This is to develop a fall-back set of skills which could secure some income should the need arise. These could be in plumbing, photography, IT-based processing, catering, or whatever. They don't have to be developed to any degree of sophistication. They will be on hand to give you confidence in your dominant career option, by ensuring a degree of security if your main strategy receives a setback.

Dick Whitcutt of Industry in Education maintains that university students need to complete a work orientation or workplace skills course alongside their degree, if they're to meet the requirements of employers. He suggests for example that the history student should gain insights into the skills required by business and industry. He suggests that an appropriate course "could lie alongside or be taken immediately after a degree".

Another angle is to set out to gather as many certificates as possible outside formal education. Learning to drive is the obvious one. But there are others that have a potential value in the workplace, like a first-aid certificate or personal counselling.

David Taylor of Anglian Water remarks on how the knowledge you acquire in one area can be applied to other areas. Anglian Water's biologists have come up with models rooted in ecosystems

to draw parallels with how tasks are carried out in human organizations. He extols the value of peeling off narrow loyalties to
individual disciplines.

Be prepared to leave your initial specialism behind, especially
if your broader experience takes you into new dimensions of
achievement and recognition. If your education in chemistry got
you a job with a glue manufacturer and you develop a flair for
generating new customers, plan some options around contributing to the marketing and promotion function.

This can also apply even before you have started using your
specialism in an employment context. Many employers in the
financial sector, for example, are keen to take on scientists and
engineers because they value the nature of the intellectual discipline that these subjects represent. A civil engineer isn't letting
the side down just because he or she doesn't build any bridges.

Consider also the options for taking on contracts running side
by side, i.e. taking a step towards becoming a portfolio worker.
The timing has to be right for this and the preparation meticu-
lous. But it's another approach to spreading the risk.

Thinking for the global market

Flexibility and adaptability arise from a state of mind rather
than innate ability. In the context of the clear advantage of generic
skills over excessive specialization, essential characteristics for
success in the global labour market include:

* letting go of any expectation that your initial learning or foundation training will see you through the rest of your life
* appreciating that learning is a continuous investment which
  replaces skills that depreciate as they approach their sell-by date
* avoiding early specialization
* establishing a firm foundation to enable you to develop a
  sequence of different high level skills as your career progresses
* being prepared for endemic change
* investing in a set of reserve skills which you can use to secure
  an income if your main career option is under threat
* working on developing your personal qualities which are
  distinct from your academic, professional or vocational pursuits
* looking out for broader experience, with the ideal being the
  multipath career

- being prepared to leave your initial specialism behind
- considering the options beyond working for a single organization
- pursuing qualifications in areas outside formal education, but with potential relevance to the workplace.

We come back to the theme of generic skills and specialization in our exploration of the digital portfolio in Chapter 7.

A price on your head: Foundations for negotiating a career investment package

If you achieve a good balance between your specialist expertise and your generic skills, you have a sound basis for negotiating with your current or potential employer an appropriate package of investments in your long-term career. But you can strengthen your position further by presenting yourself as possessing the qualities which employers constantly claim are in short supply.

There's no set formula here as employers appear unable to agree on what qualities they want and about which ones they're unable to find, especially among new or recent entrants to the labour market. In 1996 the Industry in Education network conducted some research which showed that employers were refusing to recruit many young people because they lacked the right personal qualities. The report, *Towards Employability*, stated that employers were turning to older recruits to provide the initiative and determination which they believed young people lacked – even for jobs that would suit new starters.

The report goes on: "Few young people have considered how their personal qualities and character might influence their career, believing that employers are only interested in qualifications." Dick Whitcutt finds most of the companies that Industry in Education works with, like Dixons, Vauxhall, Burtons and Midland Bank, are often disappointed with the quality of UK graduates.

The Industry in Education report also stresses the importance of "employability qualities" including diligence, proactivity and "attitude to work", all of which are difficult to measure or to demonstrate objectively. The Confederation of British Industry takes a different line, arguing the importance of "core skills" like communication, numeracy and information technology.

The Organization for Economic Co-operation and Development's experts recommend the acquisition of keyboard skills, by which it means mastery of the computer keyboard, rather than full computer literacy. The Organization also proposes the need to develop "entrepreneurial skills", among them book-keeping, pension planning and financial management.

The Association of Graduate Recruiters, which represents 300 leading UK companies, adopts yet another line. It urges graduates to develop "enabling skills", like self-promotion, networking and coping with uncertainty. Its labour market survey claims that the skills in short supply are mainly in business awareness and communication, followed by leadership and team working.

These are only a few examples of the different parameters for employability which employers' organizations have proposed. The resulting confusion has prompted the Secretary of State for Education and Employment to urge industry to get a single message across clearly, rather than their confusing brews of ill-defined qualities masquerading as a strategy for employability.

Dick Whitcutt of Industry in Education worries that words are used ambiguously in the context of the employability debate: "There's a lot said about IT being a core skill, for example. But what is it? Is it word processing? Is it understanding what's inside the box? Is it about using applications? IT is a title, like 'cup'. It's a thing – so what's the skill? These things can become just words and the meaning can be taken as different things from different perspectives."

Chris Brewster, director of the Centre for European Human Resource Management at Cranfield University, suggests that understanding of the capacity of information systems together with a knowledge of foreign languages are the distinguishing features of strong job applicants.

> OK, you can manage quite well without language skills, but if you've got them, your position in the employment market is so much stronger. If there are two people who are relatively equivalent in terms of possibility for the job and one of them has language skills, they're going to get the job because increasingly businesses are going to be international.

Despite the conflicting advice from so many organizations and individuals, once you look behind the words to trends in the recruitment and training of graduates, appropriate strategies become easier to identify. Dick Whitcutt has delivered management training to graduates who have been employed for three years or so. He has been surprised to discover how many of even the brightest graduates have been finding standard management and organizational fare a revelation.

Some trainees themselves were astonished to discover that they hadn't come across this kind of exposure to organizational dynamics at university. Oxbridge people, who might previously have thought of themselves as being at the leading edge of the labour market, were particularly shocked by this realization. But they now had an explanation they could work on to improve their standing in their companies, and hence their negotiating positions *vis-à-vis* their own career investment.

Tony Webb of the Confederation of British Industry stresses the importance of positive attitudes. In his experience, employers value an ability to adapt to change, creativity, reliability and a genuine desire to join the search for continuous improvement.

There's often a belief that employers are looking for bland and unquestioning conformity but, on the contrary, searching for continuous improvement requires skills in assertiveness and risk taking. Denise Lincoln, human resources director of Allied Domecq, doesn't surround herself with sycophants.

> I had this group of graduates together and I told them: "You just have to be prepared to take risks – even if maybe you think that's a stupid thing to do." You can't afford to be afraid of taking a challenge and learning when you do it right and when you do it badly.
>
> Then you see them around and they've got lovely personalities, but they know what they're doing and they're not afraid of going to a senior person and asking advice. That kind of bravery and confidence at the same time is important. The ability to team work and influence is a big part of business these days.

Lincoln also understands the importance of self-awareness, of people being able to work out what they're looking for from their lives and careers, of being able to balance the fact that there's more to life than just working. She accepts that this is also an important element in people going out and finding the right kind of company and the right kind of job, that will give them the kinds of opportunity that best suit their lifestyle.

She concludes that if you're selective and you join a very good company then you will find that they will help you resolve these issues. If you leave it to the company then you're letting someone else make decisions for you.

Finally, you don't have to be a genius. Lincoln is committed to broadening the skills of company employees. If they have someone who is an outstanding marketer with the ability to run a part of the business, then the company will provide the investment to improve their facility with numbers or whatever else they need to perform effectively in the new discipline.

Thinking for the global market

Paradoxically the confused messages from employers are helpful to the committed career strategist. Certainly we need to discount the outdated prescriptions like the need to develop keyboard skills. But the lack of unanimity among employers creates an opening for marketing yourself, and so the opportunity to emphasize your particular strengths and the contribution they can make to meeting the employer's objectives.

So there's no reason to despair if there are some generic skills that you find you just can't get the hang of, or if there are business-friendly personality traits that aren't part of your make-up. Go for a set of qualities which you can present as transferable, job-related, personal skills. A combination of attitudes from commitment to the customer to a disposition to solve problems, together with personal qualities like a talent for communication, team work, and organizing ability, can be packaged into a convincing offer that fits the gap which so many employers complain about.

If you're prepared to work on a range of personality assets, generic skills and positive attitudes, and to market these to prospective employers, you will have the basis from which to negotiate a career move that will incorporate a significant career development aspect within the whole package. Finally, market yourself to the companies (like Allied Domecq) which are committed to broadening their employees' skills, however talented those employees are to start off with.

Activity for the global market: A template for lifelong learning

Formal education at school is designed as a process which sorts out young people for the convenience of the labour market. The domination of public examinations taken at the ages of sixteen and eighteen illustrates how the market value of certificates is seen as more important than the content of the learning which the achievement of the certificates represents.

Simultaneously there has been an overwhelming recognition of the need for lifelong learning. Technological change is shortening the shelf life of knowledge and of work-related skills. It's also more common for people to move from one job to another, from one organization to another, from one form of contract to another. So we constantly need to update our knowledge and broaden our skills base.

This requires in turn, not lifelong education in the traditional sense of learning in a classroom setting, but exposure to learning experiences tailored to individual need and derived from different contexts. Some of these experiences will occur in a work environment. Others will comprise independent learning, the nature and content of which we design for ourselves.

The most effective way of securing a lifetime of work is for each of us to take responsibility for our own lifelong learning. We will now go through the various stages to shape a lifelong learning strategy as a continuing investment in our employability skills for the global market.

We have already addressed the issue of which directions you want to take for your career. We now need to apply those conclusions to define and deliver learning experiences that will increase your value in the global market.

We will take five aspects of personal assets which determine our performance in the workplace. These are derived from a typology produced by the organization, Industry in Education:

- knowledge and understanding
- personality traits
- skills based on knowledge
- skills based on physical activity
- personal qualities.

For each of these aspects we can make an assessment of:

- how much we need to (or have the capacity to) update, broaden or develop ourselves
- how we will go about it
- whether we want to gain some kind of formal recognition for what we achieve through our learning.

Knowledge and understanding

Knowledge and understanding in a work context are all about the information which we have acquired, processed and organized in our minds and which we draw upon in order to take action that is rational and appropriate in everyday work situations. A considerable proportion has been acquired through formal teaching reinforced by private study. Much of it is recognized through the issuing of certificates following tests and exams.

Your own assessment of the adequacy of your knowledge base will depend on such factors as how long ago you acquired it, how quickly the knowledge associated with your area of work is changing, and a number of individual factors that will apply to a greater or lesser degree to your specific work context.

You will see below a set of starter questions to launch you on course for some self-analysis. The questions aren't comprehensive, and some might not be applicable to your situation. Write down the answers to the questions you think are appropriate to you. Then define for yourself any further questions that are relevant to your current work context and record the answers to these too.

BASELINE OF WORK-RELATED KNOWLEDGE AND UNDERSTANDING

1 How quickly is the knowledge base associated with your work changing?
   •

2 How have you updated that knowledge and understanding in the past and will it be effective to continue with these methods in future?
   •

3 Do you need to gain formal recognition for the new knowledge and understanding which you are developing?
   •

4 Do you need to acquire knowledge and understanding in a related or entirely new area, either as a safeguard against the currency of your present area of expertise declining or because you have already detected that you occupy a terminal area of knowledge?
   •

5
   •

6
   •

On the basis of your reflections on these questions, you can arrive at your conclusions about how you intend to ensure that your knowledge and understanding will maintain or improve your position in your segment of the labour market. You can put these into a timeframe of, say, twelve months, and so set out your objectives for the coming year.

Learning plan: Section 1 – knowledge and understanding

For each component of learning, record how you intend to acquire the knowledge, whether you need to get your achievement accredited, and if so how (e.g. by examination, tutor or mentor reference, attendance certificate or other means).

ACQUIRING SKILLS BASED ON KNOWLEDGE AND UNDERSTANDING		
Area of knowledge or understanding	Method of acquisition	Arrangements for gaining recognition (if any)
•	•	•
•	•	•
•	•	•
•	•	•
•	•	•

Personality traits

The characteristics of one's personality constitute a problem area for work orientated self-development, because unlike personal qualities (which we will deal with later), the consensus among occupational researchers is that we're all pretty well stuck with what we were born with. Personality traits are innate and there's a limit to the extent to which we can "improve" our "performance".

That isn't to say, though, that it's sensible to ignore this whole area. For one thing, employers often put applicants for jobs through psychometric tests or aptitude profiling. Whatever you might think about the reliability of these approaches to measuring personality, it's helpful to have some idea of what they tell employers about you.

Additional sources of self-knowledge which can be useful in this context are appraisals, other forms of performance feedback (e.g. following interviews and other selection procedures) and private reflection.

These sources will give you the opportunity to present what might be interpreted as your weaknesses in a positive light at interview or to stress complementary strengths you might have. If you get the chance prior to an interview, ask for the results of any test you might be asked to complete so that you are both forewarned and forearmed.

Despite the limitations of attempts to re-engineer people's personalities, there may be some areas where you perceive weaknesses which you will be able to modify as part of your everyday work routine. If, for example, you lose patience with clients or your telephone manner lacks warmth, you can make a conscious attempt to improve your performance either by self-monitoring or by undergoing training in customer care or telephone skills.

Another approach is to analyse your strengths and weaknesses yourself and look for opportunities for more concentrated activity in your areas of weakness (if you want to improve through practice). Alternatively you might want to concentrate your effort on trying to secure the kind of work that enables you to demonstrate your strengths.

A suggestion for this element of your learning plan is set out below, though you might want to amend it to suit your own circumstances.

Learning plan: Section 2 – (a) assessing and recording personality traits

We shall begin with an assessment of your personality strengths and weaknesses. There's no need to get apprehensive about this exercise, as a weakness is often simply a strength taken to excess.

For example you might be very effective at getting things done because you're assertive or persuasive. But if you take that ability too far, you will find that you fail to achieve positive outcomes because you put people's backs up. This can be addressed by maintaining the basis of the strength, but becoming conscious of the need not to push it to extremes.

Complete the table below with as objective an assessment of your strengths and weaknesses as you can make.

ASSESSING AND RECORDING YOUR PERSONALITY TRAITS

Personality strengths (derived from own reflection, or psychometric analysis, appraisal or other sources)	Personality weaknesses (derived from own reflection, or psychometric analysis, appraisal or other sources)
•	•
•	•
•	•
•	•
•	•
•	•
•	•
•	•

Learning plan: Section 2 – (b) working on personality traits

Next select those traits that you want to work on over the next year or so. You might want to concentrate wholly on weaknesses or on strengths, or on a combination of the two. For each of the traits you choose, log how you intend to bring about the change, e.g. by attending specific training, or monitoring your own performance, or asking a colleague who works in close proximity to you to do the monitoring.

WORKING ON YOUR PERSONALITY TRAITS

Personality trait	Approach to improvement
•	•
•	•
•	•
•	•
•	•

Skills based on knowledge

Knowledge-based skills are those which enable you to communicate, to analyse and to process information in a way which adds to its value. These are at the heart of the information society. Examples are:

- literacy
- numeracy
- presentation skills
- ability to use IT
- statistical analysis
- financial analysis
- foreign language acquisition.

Although these skills constitute, to varying degrees, elements of formal education at school, college and university, they can also be developed in almost any context: at work, through independent learning, voluntary work or leisure pursuits. They can be assessed in many different ways too, for example:

- by written or oral examination leading to a certificate
- by continuous assessment as part or the whole of an award-bearing learning experience
- by workplace evaluation of completed tasks or projects, either on a formal or informal basis
- through self-evaluation.

Learning plan: Section 3 – skills based on knowledge

As in the first section of the learning plan, it will help to set out the areas of knowledge-based skills you want to acquire in the left-hand column, your learning methods in the middle column and, in the right-hand column, whether you need to gain recognition for those skills and if so through which route(s).

ACQUIRING SKILLS BASED ON KNOWLEDGE		
Skill area	Method of acquisition	Arrangements for gaining recognition (if any)
•	•	•
•	•	•
•	•	•
•	•	•
•	•	•

Skills based on physical activity

There are many areas of work which require different kinds of physical dexterity in addition to knowledge-based skills, for example:

- surgery
- engineering
- musical performance
- cookery
- physiotherapy
- craft work.

Development of these skills tends to occur on the job for those already in work, with reinforcement through instruction, observation and practice. For those aspiring to change the direction of their career to an area that requires physical skills, this is where formal instruction at an educational establishment is likely to be the most effective way of acquiring the skills. It's also likely that there will be a need for accreditation to demonstrate to potential employers that you have the requisite skills.

If this is relevant to you, then this also needs to be part of your learning plan.

Learning plan: Section 4 – skills based on physical activity

For each skill area which you complete in the left-hand column, record in the middle column how you intend to acquire the competence, whether you need to get your achievement accredited, and if so how you will do so (e.g. by examination, tutor or mentor reference, attendance certificate or other means) in the right-hand column.

ACQUIRING SKILLS BASED ON PHYSICAL ACTIVITY		
Skill area	Method of acquisition	Arrangements for gaining recognition (if any)
•	•	•
•	•	•
•	•	•
•	•	•
•	•	•

Personal qualities

Finally there is the area of work-related performance that covers one's underlying values and attitudes to work and how these become evident through what we do and how we interact with others in the workplace.

This is a more problematical area for self-development because it is so specific to one's individual work context. Someone who is naturally enthusiastic and brimful of initiative and energy in one work environment can be lacklustre or demotivated in another. Much depends on how you're treated, especially by your manager and your immediate work colleagues.

The way you're viewed by the company's management can be important in some work organizations, especially if they adopt a talent scout approach to advancement. Others, especially those in the public sector with genuine equal opportunities policies, will only promote employees on the basis of competitive selection procedures, with outside applicants having as much chance as internal ones.

That doesn't imply that in such organizations employees can be cavalier about the level of regard work colleagues have for them. But at the same time people working in such an environment are more likely to be motivated by professional pride in their work, rather than their chances of catching the eye of someone who can influence their promotion.

It's unlikely, then, that this dimension of your work will be part of a formal learning development plan. As with the section on personality traits, the discipline involves more in the way of private reflection on feedback obtained through appraisal, assessment exercises, informal evaluation of your work image and so on, and not indulgence in activities which are supposed to change your attitudes, such as company training which equates to brainwashing.

Nevertheless it is useful to take account of such feedback to assess the impact you might make at a selection interview for example. Exercises which enable you to maintain and improve your interview skills – going for interviews even for jobs that you're not interested in – will maintain your mobility in whichever labour market you're active. In addition, you need to be aware of what might be written about you in a reference to another employer.

Learning plan: Section 5 – personal qualities

Your development plan in this context, therefore, needs to focus on your work-related attitudes. Here you might wish to list the relevant attitudes, such as commitment to change, willingness to take risks, commitment to equality practices (very important in the public sector), customer orientation and, alongside these, record any evidence whereby you have displayed these attitudes.

Make a list in the left column of the work-related attitudes which are important in your work context, and next to each one record examples of your associated behaviour.

EVIDENCE OF PERSONAL QUALITIES

Work-related attitudes	Record of behaviour
•	•
•	•
•	•
•	•
•	•

This exercise will not only prepare you for some likely interview questions, but it will also focus your attention on relevant attitudes while you're engaged in your work, and thereby enable you to target your behaviour in particular directions which you will find useful to cultivate.

Thinking for the global market

Just as individuals are having to take more responsibility for their own development in the context of the workplace, so does the education system leave gaps which the global careerist needs to fill for himself or herself. The essential disciplines are:

- assessing your own abilities and weaknesses in the light of changing market conditions, both globally and in your particular area of expertise
- taking account of the concerns of employers and presenting your own skills, expertise and attitudes as a package designed to overcome those concerns
- mapping out your negotiating position with a prospective employer with a view to clinching a high-quality investment into your career strategy by the organization which secures you as its employee
- working on a career defence strategy which gives you a fall-back position in the event of your main career investment running into a dead end

- committing yourself to regular action planning, monitoring and review of your career strategy
- looking for opportunities outside your work to demonstrate abilities and personal qualities which would be attractive to an employer.

The Global Nomad

Activity for the global market: Three's a business

This chapter starts by anticipating the scepticism. I often hear the argument that, realistically, a global career can only be pursued by a small minority of high flyers; for the vast majority of employees or self-employed people, such ambitions can only fade into gauzy reverie.

I like to counter with a challenge to the sceptics to design the perfect three-person business for the global market. You try it. Use about 200 words, with the usual marketing speak as your headings:

- product
- price
- promotion
- place.

Let's throw in another heading too:

- division of labour (you've got three staff, including yourself).

THE PERFECT THREE-PERSON BUSINESS FOR THE GLOBAL MARKET

- Product
- Price
- Promotion
- Place
- Division of labour

Here's my suggested response.

THE PERFECT THREE-PERSON BUSINESS FOR THE
GLOBAL MARKET

• Product

Any service that can be delivered through use of information and communication technology, e.g. data processing, booking any kind of service, financial analysis, market research, project work.

• Price

Variable according to currency, but worked out on an estimate of time needed for the job. Aim to gross twice the average earnings level in the countries of each of the staff members.

• Promotion

Via the Internet.

• Place

Cyberspace.

• Division of labour

No specialization. Each staff member performs the same functions. Each based in countries with time zones approximately eight hours apart, e.g. Los Angeles, New Delhi and Manchester. This is a twenty-four-hour-a-day business.

There you have, in fewer than a hundred words, the standard small business of the twenty-first century. It will operate non-stop around the globe.

So here's a pretty ordinary, round-the-clock international business run by three global nomads, all spending their working hours either at home or in an office. They don't even have to travel as long as they can communicate with the rest of the world, especially with their customers and each other.

I don't need to labour the point. It doesn't have to be three people. It can be 30 or 30 000. There will always be a market for delivery of services anywhere in the world instantly, rather than having to wait until everyone's had a good night's sleep. There's a fortune to be made by the first person who sets up an agency designed to put into contact with one another threesomes from complementary time zones operating in the same line of business.

Shifting roots

Until the eighteenth century if you wanted to travel around Britain you needed to obtain permission. A trip to the next village or the town a few miles away involved you in an encounter with the local bureaucracy. For most people, if it happened at all it would be an event to remember for a lifetime.

This was all to do with the Poor Laws and the fact that each community was responsible for looking after its own poor. Each village or town, during that period, was vigilant in ensuring that no passing stranger would end up settling locally unless he or she had visible means of support. A pass told the authorities in other parts of the country which village the person on the move belonged to. This was not a society that put a premium on labour mobility.

It took the Industrial Revolution to bring that about, as the terms of trade changed and there was a vast demand for labour in the industrial heartlands of the Midlands and the north of England. For people whose families had lived in the same location for generations, the wrench was seismic. Usually they had no choice as new agricultural techniques forced them off the land and they looked for survival in the growing towns and cities.

The first generation of Britons to follow the information revolution faces choices and challenges similar to that first generation who needed to adapt to the dislocation caused by the Industrial Revolution. In one sense the offspring of the information age will find it more difficult.

Those who toiled through the Industrial Revolution were largely unskilled. They had to take their chances in the labour market of course. But they weren't required to study to gain qualifications first. They didn't have to learn new languages. The distress wasn't caused by hard times. They were used to the challenge of poverty, as their lives had previously depended on the fortunes of climate and harvest. Rather it came as a result of psychological factors associated with change of lifestyle and the pace of change.

In the twenty-first century, people will face difficult decisions about whether or not to move to find prosperity or security. Those choices will focus as much on which country they should live in, as on which town or village. The ones who lose out will be those who haven't prepared adequately.

For, although it will clearly be feasible to stay in the country of your birth, as the twenty-first century progresses it will be the case that anyone who doesn't have the confidence to live in another country, or who is unable to communicate with people overseas, will count themselves as being disenfranchised from the opportunities of the global market. It is from these people that the underclass will emerge, left behind in the struggle for work and a secure income. In the global market, mobility is the key to economic emancipation.

The nomadic lifestyle

We can expect a new style of life to spread, slowly at first but gathering speed, throughout the developed world. This is the life of the global nomad: the person who thinks nothing of moving from country to country, as we today aren't burdened with the inhibitions of our forebears in travelling and resettling around the UK.

The choice won't be a stark one, though, of staying put or being constantly on the move. There will be a menu of nomadic lifestyles to choose from. At one extreme there will be the serial nomad staying for a couple of years or more in one country after another, but eventually reaching the point where she or he no longer feels at home in the country of their birth.

At the other end of the spectrum will be the virtual nomad, who uses a networked personal computer to progress from contract to contract from a central base which acts as the nerve centre of a global communication network.

The characteristic features of the nomadic lifestyle will evolve over time, so that we can expect the following developments to occur:

• It will gradually filter down from the highest reaches of organizations.
• It will weaken individual loyalty to one particular country, but widen affinities to several.
• It will attenuate family relationships.
• In its purest form, it will create a global class of self-sufficient individuals or family units who will not think of themselves as having a home base in any one country.

Let's now examine these characteristics and their implications in more depth.

The ex-patriot: Diluting national affinities

The pull towards one particular country will weaken as the global nomad sees himself or herself as a citizen of the world, or perhaps of a large supranational entity like the European Union. They will enjoy the experience of acclimatizing to different cultural norms. They won't suffer from homesickness. They will make contact easily and build up a network of friendships outside work. These relationships will not be limited by national loyalties. Some global nomads will come to see the country of their birth as an alien environment.

Per Pundsnes is Norwegian by birth and has worked in the insurance sector in the USA and in a succession of European countries. If he were to return to Norway he would see himself seeking new contacts among non-Norwegian nationals. His experience as a global nomad enables him to "feel at home in so many different places. I would easily move to Switzerland, Germany, Holland or wherever because I have a lot of friends all over.'

On one occasion, after a two-year spell in Frankfurt which followed a period of five years spent in Zurich, as he drove from Frankfurt to Zurich he reflected upon the strength of the affinity he had developed for Zurich. He felt it strange that he, a Norwegian, should think of Zurich as his natural home.

One problem for Pundsnes is the number of times he feels constrained to respond to new contacts asking him to recount the whole of his life story from childhood. He also fears that if he does move back to Oslo, he won't feel challenged or stimulated.

Bridget Jackson, who has worked in luxury goods marketing and in the energy sector, returned to the UK after three years working in Japan. Soon after her return she caught herself looking in the mirror to verify that she was of western origin, because she had taken on so many Japanese characteristics while she had been away. It took her two years to "become English" again.

> Japanese culture is so diametrically opposed to western culture. Here it's based on appreciation and there on shame. Here it's on confidence and there on modesty. Here it's on the individual and there it's on the group.
>
> I'd taken on board all of this. I became quite diffident and kept putting myself down; I walked out of rooms backwards and I bowed all the time. I spoke in a high pitch because it's what women do out there.

When I came back, I started job searching and went to interview in several advertising agencies. As I left, I'd shake their hand and then I'd walk out backwards. I thought to myself, "you've been in Japan for too long."

There was another thing I hadn't expected: I started seeing English as a foreign language. Twice now it's happened to me. Once from Japan and once after spending some time in France. When people spoke to me in English, I would rediscover the language with so much delight. It was as though I were a child stumbling across new expressions. People would say things like "in the shake of a lamb's tail" and I'd think, "Oh! I haven't heard that for so long."

Culture clash: Alexander Rink

Alex Rink, a Canadian who has worked for several years in Portugal, provides another example of the self-sufficient, self-sustaining global nomad.

When Rink returned to Canada for a month's vacation after working for several years in Portugal, it took him a while to re-adjust. He especially remembers an early encounter with friends.

> Where it really hit home to me that I wasn't as Canadian any more was when I was at my girlfriend's cottage and we were with some other people and they were all talking little everyday things that they all recognized, but that I was completely unaware of.
>
> So for example there was a show that was very popular at the time in North America called *Friends* and they were all talking about this show and how great it was. And I had to stop them and say, "Excuse me. What are you guys talking about? What is this? Is this a show or something?"

Rink has noticed that he behaves differently in Portugal from the way he behaves in Canada.

> If you took someone who knew the two cultures and he looked at the way I operated in Portugal he would realize that it was definitely not a Canadian way of operating. And if you took the way that I deal with things

in Canada, you would see that that was definitely not a Portuguese way of doing things. So you do have to adapt certain things for the country that you're in.

That said, you have certain values that are very fundamental to you and that you would feel too threatened to change. You take along your core beliefs and you hang onto them. Those things will remain the same whether I'm in Canada, Portugal, France, or wherever I am.

Rink found his core values being assailed when he was travelling in Guatemala.

I stayed in a little beach place for a week. It was part of a Spanish school. And the people who worked there – the caretakers – they were very poor.

There was an environmental reserve nearby for sea turtles. This was on the Pacific coast. Now these sea turtles would come in and they would lay their eggs, cover them with sand and they would go back out. This is an endangered species. The government was promoting protecting the eggs and the whole area.

Now the people I was staying with invited me to dine with them and during the meal they pulled out some boiled turtle eggs. I was shocked. I couldn't believe it, coming from Canada where we're environmentally aware. And I was absolutely astounded to see them pull out the turtle eggs – like they were offering them me to eat.

I refused and at first I felt outraged. I wanted to tell them, "You absolutely can't do this. They're an endangered species" and so on. But what I realized is that these people are extremely poor and they basically have nothing else to feed themselves on. And it's very easy for someone from Canada or from England to condemn these people for what they're doing; but if you were in their situation, the chances are you would do the same thing.

It's this kind of thing that makes you identify what's truly important. My first impulse was to immediately leave the dinner table and tell them how outraged I was, maybe take the eggs or report them. But it just didn't make sense in that kind of situation.

What was so interesting about Rink and other witnesses I interviewed, was that none of them felt a sense of identity loss as a result of the distancing from their home culture which they had experienced.

Sure there was a need for some adjustment as they moved from living abroad to a period in their home country. But these were highly confident, adaptable and thoroughly engaging people who had clearly been enriched by the periods they had spent in alien cultures, and who saw returning home as simply the next in the long sequence of adaptive steps they expected to take throughout their lives.

Family division

Other models involve leaving a family behind for long periods, or weekly or monthly commuting to and from a specific base overseas. Or again, there are those who spend several months away continuously, with shorter stretches in between at home base.

A further variant is the individual with a lifelong dream. Often referred to as the migrant worker, this is the person who will spend one or more decades working abroad to build up enough capital to fulfil a lifetime's ambition at home, such as buying enough land to establish a farm.

Yet others will avoid family commitments altogether and move from contract to contract with no home base. Another approach is to take the family with you – an option which will become easier as distance learning methodologies enable children to benefit from continuity of educational provision, and as more qualification systems gain international recognition.

All these versions already exist in some form. One twentieth-century harbinger of the global nomad is the emigrant, who opts to spend a whole life in a new country. Another is the expatriate. The latter have their roots in one country, while their activity abroad in one or several countries is a staging post to be completed before they resume their career in their home country.

Much of the literature aimed at expatriates addresses the issue of how not to lose out in the career stakes when they finish their tour of duty abroad. But even that is changing: a growing feature of working abroad in the 1990s is the way that short-term assignments often turn into semi-permanent and even permanent postings overseas.

Already there are challenges to the terms we use today. Mike Peachey, personnel services manager at PowerGen, for example, casts doubt on whether it's still appropriate to describe some of those working abroad as "expatriates", given that they have no intention of returning to the UK.

So while the label "global nomad" might be new, the concept isn't. There are a fair number of these people around. And they have existed for millennia, as seafarers, merchants, mercenaries, diplomats, explorers, and in countless other occupations.

What will be new is that their numbers will increase exponentially as the technology develops to make them commonplace and as the demands of business in the twenty-first century will be such that companies will be unable to cope without a lot more of them.

Family values: Louis-Dominique Bouzy

Louis-Dominique Bouzy is of French origin and has worked with GTM Entrepose, managing large-scale engineering projects in France, the UK and Singapore. He spent eighteen months in Singapore completing his National Service. This was a special arrangement with the French government, which sends around 3000 students to different countries all over the world. They work for French companies, promoting French exports.

Bouzy was the only western person in a Malay-Chinese environment. He used English as his main language, even though at that time his English wasn't very good.

Bouzy believes that people who haven't had any international exposure in their first ten years of professional experience are at a real disadvantage. He found himself taking in the culture of each new country he was working in. For example in Singapore he had several telephone conversations in English with a Chinese business person over a number of weeks before they actually met. When they did meet, the Chinese contact was astonished to discover that Bouzy wasn't himself Chinese, because they shared identical accents.

So when he arrived in the UK he spoke English with a Chinese accent. He then went on to France where people told him he spoke French with an English accent.

Bouzy and his wife have two very young children, the elder of whom speaks English. They are concerned that, as they move from country to country, their children should develop a clear cultural identity. "I think there might be a danger with children who have travelled all over the world, especially when they're between five and fifteen. There's a balance to be found here. We've been lucky because we have strong roots in France. You can build on that and go anywhere. But you have to have your roots somewhere."

The ideal global career for Bouzy is one which allows him to intersperse a couple of years in a new country with similar lengths of time in France. He sees a global career as no more demanding than other changes of role one might expect to negotiate as part of a career. For him it's an attitude of mind: "If you get on well with people it will work out."

He urges people to start travelling from as young an age as possible, as the most effective way of gaining confidence and getting used to different cultural expectations.

The models of global nomadism will multiply. Where, for example, many expatriates rely on social networks consisting of other expatriates, others will want to become immersed in the local culture and lifestyle, and will look to develop deeper relationships with indigenous people.

It's getting more difficult to think of your future as being worked out exclusively within parochial horizons. It's not just that, for UK citizens for example, there are rights to live, work, be educated, use health systems, obtain social benefits, and so on in other countries of the European Union. Multinational companies are influencing national education systems by defining their recruitment expectations on a global scale and applying them across national boundaries. National governments are competing with each other through their tax regimes, employment laws and benefit systems to attract inward investment from global companies.

What might come as a shock to many is that this phenomenon will require planned and sustained preparation. Attitudes will have to change. Among these, as is evident from so many global careerists I have interviewed, are values associated with national and cultural identity.

Prime movers: What motivates the global nomad?

One of the delights of researching this book was the fascinating insights which witnesses from various parts of the world shared with me. I was struck by the fluidity of their thought: these were people who hadn't necessarily planned to work in a global environment, and who were still experimenting with the model of global career they wanted to adopt.

Whereas many people plan for a career that takes them outside their country of origin, others develop an international profile almost by accident. Denise Lincoln, human resources director with Allied Domecq, didn't plan to pursue a global career. She simply took the opportunities that came along and gradually broadened. "I started in a very baby way, working in a company which sent me to Germany and France quite a lot. And then from 1987, when I worked in the States with Grand Met, the job became very international. I suddenly found myself travelling a lot."

Lincoln left Grand Metropolitan in 1992 to join Laura Ashley, which has a high international profile with a multinational board. Now her responsibilities with Allied Domecq incorporate Latin America, China, Vietnam and Thailand. "So it's basically gone from just a few European countries, to cross-Atlantic, and now to Asia and Latin America. It just became more global by the day. But it was never planned that way. And yes, I love it: worldwide contacts, worldwide experience. I'm extremely lucky."

In other contexts you could find yourself in a company that suddenly develops external interests which compel employees either to adapt to working across national boundaries or to resign themselves to seeing their careers come shuddering to a halt.

The defence industry, for example, is an area where organizations are becoming increasingly networked, forming joint ventures in different countries. Often the joint venture will have an identity separate from both joint venture partners. Working in cross-functional teams thereby gains the added dimension of participation in cross-national project teams in different businesses operating to unfamiliar disciplines. The parent organizations move people between their joint ventures in different countries, often demanding flexibility of their employees up to and beyond individual tolerances.

Bridget Jackson, formerly international product manager for Alfred Dunhill and now pursuing her MBA at the INSEAD European business school, decided to pursue an international career from her early twenties because she wanted to go somewhere new and to experience something different.

> I think I had an inkling that something quite important and significant was happening in the Far East and that's where I headed.

I don't think I knew what I was expecting. I got on a plane for Japan knowing that I was going to work there for a year, but not really sure what would happen after that. I ended up in the middle of nowhere and it was really only after I had been there six months that I figured out what it meant. That's often the way I do things. I tend to make a rational decision about what I'm going to do, do it, and then deal with the emotional side afterwards.

Another of my expert witnesses is testing the feasibility of taking a break from the global career. Not all global nomads see themselves spending the whole of their lives hopping from one country to the next. Many go into this form of career knowing and intending that it shouldn't last a whole lifetime.

Susanna Wong, marketing specialist and until 1995 assistant product manager for Nestlé China, initially moved from Hong Kong to study in France. This is the first time she has been away from her family for any length of time. She doesn't plan to be internationally mobile for the rest of her life. She sees this as a career stage that's best completed while she's young.

However, Wong observes that her company, which moves its international expatriates from country to country every two to three years, doesn't make it easy to downshift back to local responsibility, other than in exceptional circumstances. Other companies are more willing to negotiate a transition from international to local working.

Diego Massidda has worked in civil engineering in Italy and South Africa, including over four years with Stewart Scott International, one of South Africa's largest consulting engineering firms. Like Susanna Wong, he has concluded that he won't always be mobile. But he's not sure whether he will settle in the country of his birth, Italy, or elsewhere.

In my last ten years I've never really planned long-term. I've always been excited not knowing what I'll be doing in a few months' time, or where I'll be. I think at some stage there will come a time when I'll be tired of this and will need more security, a more stable life, a family. At that stage I don't think I'll be as mobile.

Thinking for the global market

In the 1980s and 1990s millions of people across the developed world were perplexed and dismayed to see what they thought were secure jobs and upward careers devastated as though by a viral onslaught on an immune system. The growing internationalization of business is potentially a more benign development, especially for those who have prepared for it. As David Taylor, employment development manager with Anglian Water points out, you might need to make people redundant in one part of the business while at the same time you recruit fresh expertise for new business overseas.

Already it's not only the high flyers who undertake regular work commitments in several countries. International mobility is a requirement that has extended to the middle and even junior cadres of large numbers of companies. Many national organizations belong to global business alliances, and so even for people whose careers have progressed within the home country, demands to be flexible and move around will become more intense.

To be sure, the global career has a similar dynamic to global warming. Once begun, it creates its own energy, which causes it to accelerate. Increasingly, companies in which even a few years ago foreign travel was an experience reserved for those at board level are sending middle managers and even recent recruits on business projects overseas.

There is inexorable pressure from global companies exerted on the firms they contract with, to operate beyond national boundaries. Consequently there's a growing demand for people with the skills and experience to work in cross-national contexts. Even those who derive opportunities from their existing positions will need to have undertaken adequate preparation in order to rise to that challenge. Others will need to work at developing and demonstrating their global awareness before any opportunities come their way.

It can be a long haul. But very few of us start with a total lack of exploitable resources. The first step is to log what we have already. We will pursue this in an activity for the global market, later in this chapter.

The global recruitment genie

The sceptics argue that most vacancies can be filled locally and that international recruitment will remain a very specialized area which affects only a small minority. But evidence to the contrary is mounting. What's particularly significant is the suddenness with which companies decide to take the international recruitment route. One company after another has discovered this new treasury of talent; and once they have experienced its rewards, there's no turning back.

Anglian Water have used their commitment to internationalization as a stimulus for bringing about change across the whole organization. David Taylor, Anglian Water's employment development manager, explains: "At any time we have Anglian Water people working in various areas of the world. And we will have overseas visitors working with us in the UK. This just would not have happened a few years ago. We are starting to realize that we have to be different."

British Telecommunications is another privatized utility with a global mission. The company has a programme whereby any employee with the appropriate expertise who wants to go on a foreign secondment is considered for opportunities which arise.

Some companies use their training programmes, either in addition to or alongside recruitment policies, to enhance their global culture. Lufthansa, the German airline, for example, opted to commission Cranfield University, rather than a German provider, to deliver a development programme for their senior management. Cranfield finds large numbers of foreign companies making similar demands.

In 1996 Allied Domecq decided that they would recruit exclusively from mainland Europe in their graduate round. Their new employees originate from eight countries, with a fair proportion given assignments outside their country of origin. Each speaks three or four languages and the company sees this move as a significant contribution to its drive towards internationalization.

Denise Lincoln, the company's human resources director, is convinced that there exists now a relentless pressure towards internationalization of business. "The world becomes smaller by the day. You can see it in the UK – the cable networks being laid and technology moving by the moment. Companies are seeking out international experience and widening their supply bases. Fewer companies are willing to use recruitment consultancies that don't provide a consistent service across large numbers of countries."

Jane Kingsley, managing director of Russell Reynolds Associates, the recruitment consultancy, agrees that doing a stint abroad, on the European mainland at least, is fast becoming the norm. "People have to think much more carefully before turning down things European in their careers. There are enormous numbers of foreign companies investing over here and vice versa."

Jonathan Bratt, who manages on behalf of his company, A.C. Nielsen, a wide range of international company accounts both in the UK and on the European mainland, has noticed a greater penetration of foreign nationals into UK companies than of UK nationals into foreign companies. Jonathan Shalit, managing director of the design consultancy Sigmund Shalit & Associates, insists that a prime requirement for any company wanting to remain competitive is to attract people with a pan-European or global perspective.

By contrast, Chris Brewster, director of the Centre for European Human Resource Management at Cranfield University, has detected a reduction in cross-national movement among the big multinationals which traditionally have relied on global careers. There's more targeting of destinations, e.g. with French nationals directed towards areas of former French colonial influence.

But he has also noticed an increasing number of companies launching themselves into internationalization, and individuals going international without using the multinational corporation as part of their career plan. "They're going somewhere and finding their own job. So I think, particularly in Europe, there's no doubt that this type of activity will expand."

Musical chairs: Jonathan Stock

Jonathan Stock provides an engaging illustration of an individual who has carved out a global niche for himself without relying on the resources of an international company. He is currently pursuing an academic career in music, and is employed at the University of Durham.

His expertise is close to unique as, in addition to being a bassoon player, he has developed an in-depth knowledge of the indigenous music of China. Stock doesn't claim, though, to have planned his foray into the global market.

Stock's research in Malaysia arose from the fact that his accompanist, Joo-Lee (whom he later married), was from Malaysia. Stock followed her to Malaysia after she graduated in the UK. It struck him that being a professional bassoon player was potentially quite an isolated existence and, in any event, the competition for work was so intense that he would need to practise pretty intensively to make the grade.

Malaysia doesn't give visas to foreign husbands, other than tourist visas that last a couple of months. "So I went to the Ministry of Culture and asked them if they needed a woodwind teacher. And they said, 'OK. Fair enough.' If you write to them you never get a reply. But if you actually go in and see them, they'll arrange it there and then. So they signed me on for a tiny wage as a tutor for their National Youth Orchestra."

Stock realized that to get an academic job in music in the UK he would need a Ph.D.

> So I looked around for ideas. I found that many of my students were Chinese. Quite a few of them played Chinese folk music as well as western music. So when I was teaching them western music, I would try and get them to tell me a bit about their folk music. And that made me think: maybe I could turn these two years abroad to my advantage, and go in for non-western music.

He ended up researching ethnomusicology and Chinese music, almost by accident. His two years in Malaysia were followed by a year in China. Stock obtained a grant from the British Council. He and his wife agreed that, because the grant was modest, he should go on his own.

The preparation was detailed, including learning some Mandarin Chinese and taking lessons on the Chinese two-stringed fiddle. "It was just enough to give me some kind of proficiency. At least it meant I knew how to hold the thing and play a folk song or two. And that was enough to be able to go to teachers in China and say, 'Look I can do this. What else do I need to learn?'"

Stock's studies entailed his asking Chinese people about the traditions associated with the two-stringed fiddle and what the attractions of playing it were. He also wanted to know what influence the government had had over the development of folk traditions.

I suppose as far as the college was concerned, the Shanghai Conservatory of Music, I was a performing student and therefore I was there to get lessons and they weren't particularly interested in the rest. If I wanted to go round asking funny questions that was my business.

Accommodation was provided for Stock in a student hall of residence. "They weren't too keen that I should mix and contaminate the locals, but they ended up pretty relaxed about it."
Getting a reasonable meal presented a bigger challenge.

I managed to get permission to go to the Chinese students' canteen, which they weren't too keen on. They used to make jokes about "Big Nose is here again". Big Nose is the word for foreigners. They felt that foreigners had their own foreign students' canteen and we should really go there. The problem was the foreign students' canteen didn't have a very good cook. His stuff was disgusting.

Stock took every opportunity to talk to people on the streets. "This was something that the Conservatory people found strange because they said, 'Look we've given you a teacher who is a professor. He's an expert. So why do you want to interview people outside?' They couldn't understand this idea of getting a survey of different opinions on things."
Now that he has returned to the UK, Stock sees himself as a stronger and more flexible person, and much broader in outlook. "It's often a reminder that there are different ways of achieving ends and people have their own ways of doing things."
Jonathan Stock's experience demonstrates how someone with little prior knowledge of living or working on the other side of the world can lay down the foundations of his career without the resources of a multinational company or other organization to support him. It provides another illustration of the diversity of approach to, and realization of, the lifestyle of the global nomad.

Thinking for the global market

Much of the evidence is anecdotal, but it still indicates that opportunities to work in international environments are being taken up more vigorously by new entrants to the labour market from the European mainland than by those from the UK.

One practical response, which will extend the international focus of your thinking beyond the immediate project itself, is to research the different expectations of companies in various European countries and beyond, of how they expect CVs to be set out and what they should contain. Many university careers services have samples of different European CVs and American résumés.

German employers, for example, expect brevity and concision in CVs, and favour candidates with a broader approach to business, rather than an emphasis on a particular specialism. If you can offer marketing and strategic skills in addition to your specialism, you will have an advantage. The larger companies usually take on management recruits immediately they graduate, and then train them further in-house.

Scandinavian countries tend to pay less attention to formal qualifications. They're more interested in personal qualities. At the other extreme, in France quality of degree and the institution attended are considered very important. Dutch companies usually look for management recruits whose first degrees are in subjects such as business and engineering. They aren't very impressed by degrees in arts subjects.

Terry Caine of the Overseas Placing Unit suggests that if you want to apply for a job in a member state of the European Union, you should use the local language. If you use a translator, then make it clear that you have done so, to avoid problems and potential embarrassment at interview.

Mick Carey, director of Careers Europe, maintains that there are exceptions. One is if the job is advertised in a language other than the local one: this usually indicates that the company is looking for a cross-national dimension. In these circumstances, an application in English would be acceptable.

Another exception is where the company operates in the international market and adopts a common working language. An oil company based in the Netherlands with interests in the Middle East or offshore America, for example, is likely to use a working language other than Dutch.

Companies active in eastern Europe are also more likely to accept CVs or portfolios written in English, particularly where they are keen to recruit to particular specialisms which will be in short supply among local business people.

Careers Europe will track down specimen CVs from various European countries to give potential applicants an idea of local expectations.

A second strategy relates to a potential self-marketing angle. One aspect of working on specific international assignments, even from within your normal workbase, is that they take so much longer to complete than the equivalent activity in your home country. Just getting hold of people in several countries and across time zones can be time-consuming. You need to take account of traditional holiday seasons, for example. Most of all there's the necessity to cater for cultural behaviours where these place other values above getting the job completed.

Activity for the global market: Recording your cross-cultural experience

Many companies invest huge resources into preparing their staff for overseas projects. Thus there's advantage in logging every kind of cross-cultural business experience you have had, and showing the benefit to the company or potential recruiter. It could be something as simple as demonstrating that you understand the need to gather as much information as you can, including the particular way that business is done in an overseas part of the organization, before you go on a foreign assignment.

Here's a format you can use to record that experience. Use the left-hand column to log examples of your cross-cultural and international experience, and the right-hand column to assess the business applications of that experience.

RECORD OF CROSS-CULTURAL OR INTERNATIONAL EXPERIENCE

Example of cross-cultural or international experience	Potential application or significance to a company
•	•
•	•
•	•
•	•
•	•

New model nomads

At first sight the figures on cross-national migration would seem to dampen predictions about the exponential growth of global careers involving permanent relocation. The World Development Report suggests that migration is the laggard among all the elements of globalization, with the trend actually falling.

Migration between industrial countries has fallen from 2.5 people per 1000 inhabitants in 1970, to 1.5 per 1000 in 1990. In addition, most migrants stay within their region. The annual migratory flows from developing to developed countries, at 1 immigrant per 1000 inhabitants, is about the same as it was in 1970.

The European Commission's latest figures show that, although 4.3 per cent of its citizens live permanently outside their home country, only about 2 per cent of the total workforce work outside their home country.

Altogether about 1.5 per cent of the global labour force work outside their home country. General labour mobility has been constrained by institutions, culture and xenophobia.

However it's clear that official figures understate the extent of relocation between countries for the purposes of pursuing work contracts. Such contracts typically last well under three years. You can be "based" in the UK, but still move from contract to contract or pursue other forms of international career without this being shown up in migration statistics.

There is also a historical movement towards increasing inter-dependence of the labour force on a global scale. This is being brought about by three factors:

- global employment in the multinational corporations and the cross-border networks which arise in their wake
- the impact of international trade on employment and working conditions, both in the north and the south
- the effects of global competition and of the adoption of flexible management practices on each country's workforce.

All three developments are driven by advances in IT, which create the linkages between different segments of the labour force across national boundaries.

Another aspect of globalization that's often understated is the existence of traditions of emigration and ethnic networking across the world. The Nordic countries, for example, enjoy a long tradition of people moving from one country to another. There are strong affinities between emigré communities and compatriots in their home countries.

Perhaps the most dynamic example of the operation of a powerful economic network based on ethnicity is the Anglo-Chinese community. The term applies to five million or so better-educated Chinese who not only know English but are fluent in (Cantonese) Chinese as well. Many have settled in North America, the UK, Australasia, the West Indies, and the south Pacific as well as south-east Asia.

In the global market, bilingual Anglo-Chinese have found it easy to participate in international trade. The growth of Hong Kong and Singapore as commercial and financial centres and their links with cities where Chinese are also strongly represented, like London, Manila, San Francisco, New York, Toronto, Vancouver, Sydney and Melbourne, all confirm their global strength.

The Anglo-Chinese also enjoy a cultural sophistication through their knowledge of and sensitivity to two civilizations. The cultural traffic is now two-way: gone is the time when the Anglo-Chinese were merely channels for Anglo-American values exported to China. They now offer understanding of Chinese traditions and values in the reverse direction, to be appreciated by the English-speaking world and beyond.

Another social trend which is well advanced in the western world will create the space for many to enhance their global competitiveness. This is the rise of single person power.

This phenomenon is one of the most powerful forces shaping industrialized societies. The evidence from the UK alone is over-whelming, with manufacturers and retailers changing goods and services to suit single people. Research by Mintel, the market research group, suggests that the number of people living alone in the UK will have risen to eight million by the year 2000, with the most rapid growth among those under the age of thirty-five. Nearly two-thirds of single women and 54 per cent of single men are in the most affluent ABC1 income group.

That creates a more mobile society than we have been used to, and clearly one which is ready for the growth of global nomadism. These singles will find it easier to uproot and find work at the other end of the country, or the other end of the continent. Similar trends are apparent in other European Union countries. We can expect more European singles coming to live in the UK and competing for jobs.

New and potential entrants to the labour market are expressing greater expectations in terms of pursuing mobile careers. When *The European* newspaper conducted a survey of fifteen to twenty-five year olds across Europe, it found that more than four-fifths of young people said they would go abroad to find work. Highfliers Research found that, of over 10 000 graduates leaving twenty-four UK universities in 1996, one in five said that they wanted their first job outside the UK.

Colm Tobin of the careers service at University College Dublin sees increasing numbers of the more able graduates opting to work abroad, with the European mainland as well as the UK and the USA being the favoured destinations. Twenty per cent of Irish graduates now find employment overseas after they have finished their studies.

Tobin observes: "The young people we see these days not only feel the need to be adapted to international mobility, but they actually love the idea. It's rare to come across a student at our universities in Ireland who doesn't spend at least one summer abroad and possibly two or three – often both in the United States and in Europe".

Record numbers of Swedish students are seeking places at foreign universities. Stefan Amer, chair of the Swedish National Union of Students, is confident that numbers studying abroad will double within five or ten years. Currently about 20 per cent of Swedish students spend time abroad as part of their degree course.

Cranfield University is one of many business schools which now feature internationalization heavily in their MBA programmes. A high proportion of completers go on to international careers, even though for most of them the whole of their previous career was only nationally focused.

Since its launch in 1990, more than half a million young Europeans have taken advantage of the Socrates (formerly Erasmus) scheme of inter-university ties and travel bursaries, to study abroad for up to six months. With the programme now extended to include secondary school students, the European Commission expects that by the year 2000 one in ten students could be studying abroad.

Other programmes include the Youth for Europe initiative, to enable young volunteers to undertake community service projects outside their own country, both inside and outside the European Union. The European Voluntary Service for Young People programme is aimed at those between the ages of eighteen and twenty-five undertaking voluntary work in Europe for between six and twelve months.

The Euro qualification programme is designed to give the opportunity to young people to work in transnational business partnerships, or to achieve personal vocational mobility within the European Union. The programme is open to those under the age of twenty-five who are seeking a job, or those over twenty-five who have been unemployed for a year or more. The training is available across forty occupations, ranging from restoration of ancient buildings to heavy goods vehicle driving (internationally).

Professor Chris Brewster's research at Cranfield University has found two basic sorts of people moving around the world, with one at each end of the income scale. He characterizes the labour market in Europe as international at the very top and at the very bottom, with the middle section remaining fundamentally national.

For high-flying managers and top specialists, the international arena is the place to be. Very senior managers and professional people are happy living in cosmopolitan cities like Brussels, New York and Paris. It really doesn't make that much difference to their lifestyles and they have come to regard it as a natural part of the process of pursuing a career.

The other cross-nationals are people on building sites, in cleaning companies, in hospitals as porters and security staff, many of whom feel that they might as well be anywhere in any case, because nobody ever talks to them. They're attracted by the income levels: a Portuguese porter in Switzerland will earn more than they would in most jobs they might have access to in Portugal.

There are also inhibiting factors such as comparability of qualifications. Some countries in the European Union, for example, cynically exploit loopholes in regulations in order to restrict free access to employment opportunities. But even such practices as the German insistence that teachers must be civil servants who, by definition, must be German citizens, aren't as restrictive as the visa and work permit regulations of two decades ago.

Over half the beneficiaries of the European Union directive on the recognition of diplomas originate from the UK. Although implementation has been slow, an accelerating number of professionals who are fully qualified in one member state are practising that profession in another.

Although there will continue to be problems in relation to the standardization of qualifications in areas like engineering and medicine, information technology is likely to promote speedier conformity of standards of qualifications in areas like accounting and banking, where computer software is establishing a consistency of definition and practice internationally that was unimaginable even ten years ago.

Even so, there is still a way to go before we can accept the insight from economics that people, unlike land and capital, constitute the most flexible factor of production. But the fundamentals of those economics are changing too, in a way that will have a permanent effect on career structures even outside the developed economies.

New trade winds

From colonial times to the end of the 1980s, there has been a linear relationship between the developed economies and the developing ones. Growth in the northern hemisphere has brought about good times for the south, as the latter has been dependent on exports to the developed economies. However, the synchronization between recession in the north and deceleration of growth in the south broke down in the late 1980s.

Since then, reverse linkages have become increasingly apparent, from the economies of the south to those of the north. Exporters in the north are more dependent on growth in the economies of the south (especially those of south-east Asia), and the latter no longer rely on the rate of growth of the northern economies.

One reason for this growth, in addition to trade liberalization and structural reforms introduced into some southern economies, has been the huge increase in capital investment. Capital flows from north to south have increased significantly since the late 1980s, and for the first time much of this investment is private capital, reflecting the desire of investors to go outside their own slow-growing economies.

This foreign investment has contributed to giving the newly industrializing Asian countries access to advanced production technology and a broader export base within a relatively short time. Overseas investment by northern multinational companies has grown much more quickly than imports and exports, and this trend illustrates what many commentators see as the central characteristic of globalization: the growth of investment rather than of trade.

This has led to increasing demands for a wider definition of free trade, to allow not only the right to ship goods across borders without artificial barriers, but the freedom to set up businesses on equal terms within a country's borders. Markets will be contested as much by direct access as by trade.

The implications for freedom of access to employment opportunities in countries throughout the world are breathtaking. It is a liberalizing development which, once begun in earnest, will be irreversible. Its most noticeable effect will be to make the international career the rule rather than the exception.

At present the barriers to doing business by investment are legion. Not only are they often deeply embedded in a country's culture, but tax systems, labour laws, environmental standards and national competition policies all reinforce them.

For service industries the obstacles are more intense than for manufacturing, particularly when it comes to opportunities allowed for non-nationals to work for a company which needs their expertise. It is these barriers, of course, that explain the low figures we saw earlier in the chapter of those people working permanently in other countries. The Organization for Economic Co-operation and Development intends to tackle free trade in services and investment as the next big challenge in global initiatives in trade liberalization.

Within the European context, the introduction of the single currency will have a significant impact on cross-border careers, for all member states – even the ones which might retain their own currencies. The pressure for businesses to operate from within the single currency area will create a huge impetus to diversify the employee bases of companies. One prospect is the creation of a golden triangle in the middle of the European Union, with the peripheral regions becoming less attractive as business and career prospects.

For the individual, signing up to a contract with a known currency value will be a magnetic incentive to work from within the single currency area. The longer-term attractions of building up savings and pension contributions in a currency that's unlikely to depreciate also shouldn't be underestimated. Any country deciding to stay out of the single currency will give its most talented people every reason to relocate to Europe's centre of gravity.

Other countries will face individual challenges that could also accelerate the globalization of careers. One example is Singapore, which faces a policy dilemma because of its high rates of growth. This may require increased importation of foreign workers at all levels including senior managers. The number of skilled professionals from India and China working in Singapore has increased dramatically in the past few years and the government is keeping the door wide open for foreign skilled workers.

Another feature of globalization that has attracted attention is its complementarity with the trend for flatter organizational structures. With work becoming more project based and team oriented with flexible boundaries, international experience is seen by recruiters and potential recruits alike as convincing preparation for working effectively in organizations that prize interpersonal and networking skills, autonomy (within teams), and a desire to learn.

In the early years of the next century we can expect professional associations to be organizing themselves on a worldwide basis. Members working in successive countries will be supported by organizations that can meet their needs for acquiring accommodation, establishing social networks, keeping links with their home base, and building on the affinities they will have with other professionals pursuing a similar lifestyle. They will provide assistance on health, insurance, the education of their children, the career patterns of their partners, and further investment in their own skills and knowledge.

Thinking for the global market

The evidence is that globalization is an accelerating phenomenon. Jane Kingsley of Russell Reynolds Associates is convinced that people's preferences will not be the determining influence over the rate at which the incidence of global careers will expand. "If the economics points that way, then it will just happen."

Eryl McNally MEP considers it "very foolish" for anyone not to spend some time working abroad: "If you feel happier in an English-speaking country like the United States or Australia, then that at least gives you the idea that you can do things differently. But better still is working in a country with a different language. If you want to get ahead in the global economy, go and get a job in another country."

The challenge is, of course, to prepare properly. Going on a study visit abroad, for example, gives you much more than the experience itself. It heightens your analytical skills and broadens your imagination as you see things done differently abroad, encounter organizations operating within unfamiliar cultures and come across distinctive expectations and values.

The fact that you're on a European Union scheme doesn't mean that you don't have to prepare properly either. A number of students return each year with horror stories about their experiences. One reason why foreign students study in the UK is that there's a better standard of teaching and pastoral care than in most other European higher education systems.

The nightmare for some exchange students from the UK has been a spell at a European mainland university with no laboratory work, no lecturers turning up, several hundred people trying to squeeze into a lecture theatre and the accommodation they were promised falling through.

If the conditions are right, though, then as well as encouraging greater reflection, experience in a foreign country is critical to an appreciation of cultural differences, which itself is vital to successful teamworking in the global market.

Another route to cross-cultural experience is through short-term working abroad. Even a low-skills job can help you develop an insight into another country's culture, as well as providing the opportunity to practise the relevant language. It also enables you to find out about the local employment market.

One key investment for the future, then, is in our mobility skills. We have seen how even adjacent regions can diverge significantly in economic performance. If there's no future in being tied to the village, town or country where you were born, you need to have the experience and confidence that enables you to move successfully.

Yet even at the simplest level of mobility, only one in five Britons has ever driven abroad according to a survey of international motorists carried out by Europe Car Interrent. That compares with 90 per cent of Swiss and 80 per cent of Belgians.

There are plenty of books which provide advice on how to get a job in a particular part of the world. For short-term job and work experience opportunities, these are worthwhile, but the global career strategist needs to adopt a more long-term approach. One route is to get recruited by a company in your home country that provides opportunities to work abroad.

Of the Times Newspapers UK top 100 companies, at least twenty employ the majority of their workforce abroad. Many others are moving in this direction as investment overseas increases. Some major UK companies now have domestic operations which are of marginal importance compared to the global context in which they operate.

Opportunities to work and study abroad have never been greater. There are programmes not only for students and those in work, but also for the unemployed, to enhance their chances of working outside their home country. It's essential to get this kind of experience as early as possible, to ensure that you keep your options for the longer term as open as possible.

The art of global communication

If you want to pursue a global career, you will need to have skills in global communication. This is an area ripe with polemic, especially about the value of English as the language of international business. It's difficult to draw general conclusions, because so much depends upon the aspirations and circumstances of the individual.

If, for example, you intend to engage in a global career from your personal computer, modem and Internet connection, you won't need advanced or specialist communication skills unless you're in a niche market like marketing Indonesian gamelans.

What's important here is to assess the context of your career in the light of the need for communication skills that go beyond which language you use, to being able to respond appropriately to different cultural expectations. We shall examine these issues next, in particular:

- the extent to which you can rely on English as the language of international business
- the role of translators and interpreters, and of translation software
- the challenge of working across cultural barriers.

Conversation stopper 1: Everyone speaks English

There has been a vigorous debate about whether an ability to speak one or more foreign languages is an essential requirement for an international career. On current evidence it's clear that you can pursue a global career from a single language base: there are many who do so already. But our focus is on the future and so we need to examine the arguments in more depth and in the context of the developments that we have already examined.

Some argue that because English is the language of international business, those who have English as their first language are privileged in that they don't have to learn other languages. There can even be disadvantages to speaking the local language, as Jonathan Stock discovered when he started speaking the local language in Malaysia.

> By insisting on speaking Malay to them you were infer-
> ring that they didn't have a good education. So it was
> really only with people who couldn't speak English that
> I learnt to use Malay.

One counter-argument draws attention to the nature of international English. Some observers have noticed that in a mixed national group where English is used as the common language, some participants find it easier to converse with other non-first-language speakers of English rather than with first-language speakers. This is because they share an emerging variety of English which almost equates to a foreign language to the first-language English speaker.

Per Pundsnes, whose first language is Norwegian and who has worked in the insurance sector in the USA and in a succession of European countries, has found that in some countries the local people like to practise their English. "On the other hand, I feel that they show a lot of respect if you're able to just give them the impression that you care about knowing the local language."

He believes that where he uses English because he doesn't know the local language, he's viewed differently from a first-language English speaker because he is communicating in what to him is a foreign language, with another foreigner. "Speaking in English to a non-mother tongue English speaker puts us on the same level as we're both making an effort."

There are large numbers of business people who have developed high-order skills in English as a foreign language and who can easily make themselves understood, indeed whose use of English can rival and surpass that of first-language speakers. There's no doubt, then, that effective communication does go on in English between people of different national backgrounds.

The debate about the use of English in international business circles has moved on from questions about the mechanics of communication, to issues concerned with subliminal messages about quasi-colonial superiority and attitudes to diversity of culture. (It's for that reason that I use the term "first-language speaker", in preference to the more conventional "native speaker", which has potentially offensive connotations.)

Stephanie James of the British Chambers of Commerce stresses the importance of a knowledge of languages as an aspect of customer care in the global market. "It's not all based on price now; it's all based on quality and backing up and going back to the customer and part of that is that if you can speak German and you're dealing with a German company, then that can be the difference between a sale and a non-sale."

The ability to use another language is also essential to get behind the words and develop an appreciation of the way others think. The absence of foreign language skills compromises awareness of the subtleties of operating in an international environment.

Alex Rink, currently studying at the INSEAD European business school in Fontainebleau, has noticed how much better he understood his Portuguese colleagues when he could speak the language. "The more I learnt the language, the better I understood the people. Some of their expressions speak volumes about their national psyche."

Christopher Bissell, head of department of telematics at the Open University, remarks how people might say something to you in one language which they wouldn't dream of saying in another. A German colleague he met at a conference confessed that he had a lot of problems with English students for various reasons.

> It became clear that it was a big cultural thing because being a student in Germany is not like being a student in Britain. For a start they're older, they might be married and have all sorts of commitments. You don't treat it like being a big game. There was obviously a culture clash here.
>
> The interesting thing about this is that he was very frank about it. So frank that the next morning, at breakfast, he came up to me and apologized, I guess because he felt he'd been rude. But I think that had we been speaking English, he wouldn't have shared these views with me. I think the fact we were speaking German

made it natural for him to talk about these cultural issues in German, which I don't think he would have done in English. Understanding that sort of thing is very important for business negotiations.

Eryl McNally is an accomplished linguist as well as being a Member of the European Parliament. She has noticed that first-language English speakers who don't have an understanding of communication developed through learning a foreign language will use idiomatic expressions which non-first-language English speakers don't understand. As a result they often leave the discussion oblivious to the negative feelings they have generated.

Dick Whitcutt, director, Industry in Education, is optimistic about the opportunities available to English speakers even if they don't speak a foreign language fluently. He cites the large numbers of consultants and senior managers who have gone to eastern Europe and Russia, where language had previously been a major obstacle.

He also argues that, in the Netherlands for example, there are so many multinational companies using English as the everyday language that this doesn't create an insuperable barrier. Some multinationals in Germany and Switzerland also have English as the common language. "Even though others are getting better at English, there will still be an opening up to English speakers for a long time. I accept that when the whole world speaks fluent English, which will possibly come one day, any comparative advantage will be lost."

Use of foreign languages develops relationships and opens up communication well beyond first base of just getting the content of your message across. It indicates openness, respect, flexibility, confidence and equality. It's also immensely powerful as a marketing device.

In the short to medium term, then, global opportunities are being opened up to first-language English speakers, but the competition for them will intensify over the longer term. The global careerist will look to take advantage of the immediate opportunities while they last, but may also need to invest in other languages to maintain that edge into the future.

Conversation stopper 2: You can use an interpreter

Another potential refuge for those reluctant to develop foreign language skills is the world of translators, interpreters and

translation software. There are certainly occasions when there's
no alternative to the use of interpreters. Business people themselves, though, are aware of the barriers to personal communication which interpreters can create, as well as the scope for
misunderstanding of non-verbal cues, which even the most accomplished interpreter can't overcome.

Less is left to chance with written communication. Even accomplished speakers of foreign languages will use translators for
significant documents. Translation software for use with written
communication has also developed considerably during the past
decade, especially for language pairs which include English. The
European Commission, for example, uses the Systran system,
which now covers seventeen language pairs.

In its early years, the system was subject to a computer-
generated sense of humour with the French-English translation
of the phrase "*vis-à-vis*", for example, coming out as "live to
screw". But improvements in computer processing power and
extensions to the system's phrasal dictionary have reduced the
error rate.

There are no systems, though, which can operate without
human intervention. It wouldn't be wise to make any plans that
assume that high-quality written translation – let alone simultaneous oral translation – will become available even within decades.

Gaining in translation: Rory McMahon

Rory McMahon works for a fast-expanding European packaging
business. McMahon travels throughout eastern Europe, from
Russia and the Baltic states to Bulgaria. He speaks only English
but uses local staff to interpret for him. "When I travel the local
office manager comes with me and he does the translating. When
I speak to customers I give them technical knowledge and direct
contact with the company about our products, whether that's for
a marketing or sales function."

McMahon doesn't see his inability to use languages as a
problem.

> When I go to places like Russia and the more eastern
> countries, they're so pleased to see someone from the
> west, so grateful that you've made the effort to go there.
> So language isn't an issue at all. They're happy to use

a translator: it's the normal mode of communication for them.

You can make the fact that you're using a translator work for you, like using the time to give yourself longer to think. If the translator is yours, then you can control the meeting much better because you have a relationship, and experience that builds up.

You both know which way you want the meeting to go. You prepare tactics together beforehand. You can use your translator to stall a meeting. If you need time to think you can say you didn't quite understand that and it will take a minute for that question to come back again in which time you've thought about the ramifications.

It takes a couple of months to get used to using a translator. The first visit with a new translator is difficult and some you have to keep a hold of because they're not employed as translators, they're just technical people. What you have to keep a hold on is that they actually do say what you tell them. You have to keep a tight rein on them, but in a friendly way as well, because you need long-term commitment from them.

You begin to pick up words. You can feel the sense of what's being said. And you see all the non-verbals, the body language, and of course if you talk for a minute and they only take ten seconds to translate it, you realize that something's not being communicated. If you only give a short answer and they carry on for ages, you know they're adding their own gloss.

Although communication in English or via an interpreter can work in some circumstances, it's evident that as the global economy impacts increasingly on our lives and the global career becomes the rule rather than the exception, then the younger you are the more likely it is that you will need to communicate in languages other than English.

The role of English as an international language creates a uniquely Anglo-Saxon reluctance to pursue the acquisition of foreign languages. The European Commission promotes the learning of at least two European Union foreign languages by all young people. Several European Union countries go beyond that standard, launching children on learning foreign languages from as early as six years of age.

Children in most UK schools start learning foreign languages later than their counterparts on the European mainland, study fewer of them, spend less time on them and can drop them earlier. The choice of language is determined by teacher supply rather than the diversified requirements of the global economy.

In Luxembourg, eighteen to twenty-four year olds speak an average of 2.7 foreign languages per head. The figure in Denmark is 1.8 and the Netherlands 1.6. The UK average is 0.5. Sixty-one per cent of this age group in the UK can't speak a foreign language. The equivalent figure in Denmark is 2 per cent. In the Netherlands it is 6 per cent.

Many mainland European businesses understand the role of language skills in maintaining competitiveness. Eighty-five per cent of mainland European students under twenty-five learn English as their second language. You can find English of remarkable quality spoken by students in universities in the Netherlands and Norway. The standard of English spoken by many mainland Europeans is now so good that it can match the best-educated first-language speakers of English.

Even though he believes that people can get by almost anywhere with English, Rory McMahon, marketing manager with a European packaging company, advises people coming onto the labour market to develop their language skills. He cautions, though, against ignoring local prejudice as far as his sphere of operation – eastern Europe – is concerned.

> Poles and Russians don't like the Germans and don't particularly want to speak German even if they can.
>
> You can get by very well with German in Slovakia and the Czech Republic. If you use Russian – they all speak Russian but again you've got this problem with the Poles being hostile towards Russian. They would say, "Well, why are you learning Russian when you should be learning Polish?"

In Asia too, particularly because of the global influence of the United States, the use of high-quality English is spreading. Malaysia and China have launched drives to encourage students to acquire higher standards of English. In commercial cities such as Hong Kong, Bombay, Shanghai, Tokyo, Kuala Lumpur, Jakarta and Bangkok, and in the city state of Singapore, the demand for professionals with higher standards of English is increasing. Chambers of Commerce across the Pacific Rim are urging the need to employ teachers of English to lift standards to enable businesses to perform more efficiently and extensively.

The significance of this spread of high-quality English is the impact it will have on recruitment in the global labour market. This is a crucial lesson for those who want a secure future in the global market. Because of the timescales involved, companies are more likely to recruit people with language skills already than to invest in training them. Only 7 per cent of UK employers currently organize foreign language training for their employees.

The wealth of nations: Cross-cultural collaboration

Another aspect of the ability to communicate globally is the fascinating and potentially personally rewarding area of sensitivity to cultural differences, especially in the context of the increasing phenomenon within the global market of working in multicultural teams. Cross-cultural capability is a powerful source of career and business advantage.

Even those who do not pursue global careers intentionally will become increasingly exposed to the challenge of working with people from different national and cultural backgrounds, whether as colleagues, customers or suppliers. Being able to handle that kind of relationship is now essential for success in business.

Much of the literature on global business culture consists of lists of shallow and generalized cultural do's and don'ts applied to individual countries. The implication is that if you mimic certain behaviours, you will succeed.

But the challenge of working successfully across cultures is much more intricate. You have to:

- win the respect of those who have different values
- reconcile difficulties arising from apparent contradictions
- interpret ambiguities
- behave more intuitively than many of those brought up in western societies are used to.

Global careerists need practical experience of working in cross-cultural teams and in unfamiliar cultural contexts in order to develop their awareness and skills.

Denise Lincoln, human resources director at Allied Domecq, gained her first experience of multicultural working in the prosaic environment of a Slough industrial estate, working for Bestobell

Seals. The company employed 400 people from different national and cultural backgrounds.

> You had Muslims and Sikhs, Bangladeshis and Polish people.
> I worked with them on the shop floor and got a great understanding. It gave me a big awareness of people's differences. That's helped me enormously now I'm in a job where what's important more than anything is to appreciate the differences between individuals, and that people's psychological make-up is different.

Subsequently she worked with the multinational firms, Rank Xerox and Grand Metropolitan, lived in the United States and came to realize that "although the language was very much the same, the cultures were very different from what I could possibly have expected from over here. And then spending time working in places like Japan, where clearly the language and the cultural barriers are so great, and the way in which you do business is very different."

Lincoln places the challenge of preparing individual employees for the norm of working in cross-cultural teams within the broader context of understanding diversity. She believes this applies as strongly to developing sensitivity to differences of behaviour and expectations associated with gender, as it does to culture.

She also sees the issue extending to age and to disability.

> Very often you hear people say that the human resource side of things is soft, the soft side of business. And I always stand up to remarks like that and say it's nothing of the kind. If you describe it as soft then I know what you mean, but actually it's hard. And it's the hardest thing that you can do but you can succeed as long as you're prepared to invest.
> Teams don't just happen. We have to invest a lot in people's experience, in team work and in under-standing. You certainly get the payback if you do it.

As a woman she has found it difficult to work in some cultures where women aren't seen as naturally having a role in business. She has had to think carefully about her approach.

> If you do the male thing which is to get very aggressive, you can't win. If you do the female thing which is to

absorb it and let it fly over you, that's not right either. But I think that's probably the better option. You have to understand what's happening.

But usually people are fine. It's funny sometimes to go to some cultures. In Mexico, for example, and in Japan, it's quite funny to go there. They know they have to treat you properly, but it's all a bit new to them.

Lincoln finds endless rewards in her work of shaping teams.

One of the most delightful things I've seen in Allied Domecq is the European team working together, which is a truly pan-European team including a Polish guy, someone from what used to be the eastern bloc, and it works extremely well. There's a lovely camaraderie between them.

And they're alike inasmuch as they're true polyglots. They can speak to each other in six or seven languages. They're as happy in their country as they are in another and they appreciate that although this one might be a Brit, they have the same understanding of different countries. They don't feel that they're talking to a Brit who hasn't a clue. It's wonderful to be in on that.

Richard Steele, management consultant with Marakon Associates, considers adaptability in terms of understanding other cultures and modes of operation as a core skill. "You can never overestimate the cultural differences between European countries. The subtleties are enormous."

He finds that cross-cultural groups often polarize.

Sometimes you just accept that you can't reach a consensus. People look at the time that it's taken to get so far. You just have to accept that you can't bring everybody with you.

There's a law of diminishing returns that's operating here. If there are three or four perspectives, it's useful. Eight is just impossible. There must be an optimum number. And any one person can screw it up. I've done it myself – it comes as a bolt from the blue when I found out I was the one causing all the resentment.

There was a German guy who was always riding roughshod over an Israeli woman in the group. I noticed it and I thought that she had a lot to contribute. And I was always trying to promote her and say, "Well why don't we listen to Tama for a while?" or "What a good point," to try to reinforce it. And her feedback to me was, "Don't patronize me. I'll fight my own battles."

And it turns out that she's trained Israeli fighter pilots at the top fighter academy in Israel and she's done three years military service and she can stick up for herself basically. She doesn't need some English idiot to intervene.

Rory McMahon, international marketing manager, accepts some of the national stereotypes, but stresses the importance of adaptability.

I work with a cross-European team, so there'll be Francesco from Italy, Willem from Belgium, Delphine from France, a Dane and a German, and of course everyone is very different. We know that Francesco will take ages and gesticulate all over the place. And you know the German will be very structured, maybe cautious in his approach, but with a lot of research behind it.

And you adjust to all of these and see the advantages. I think as long as you don't go in there as the Basil Fawlty type person – "I'm British, I've got my bowler hat on and I'm not going to change for anyone else and everyone else has got to act British. We were the Empire." – as long as you go in there to take everyone at face value you'll find that you don't have to adjust yourself too much, but just be aware of other people's cultures so that you can filter the information within your terms.

When Susanna Wong moved from Hong Kong to France, she felt guilty because she didn't have to work as hard as when she had been in Hong Kong. "Then I said, 'OK. This is the way people work here. If you push too hard, you create pressure and make things worse.'" She found life easier when she accepted the prevailing norms.

Jonathan Stock, lecturer at Durham University, provides an appealing metaphor on the challenge of understanding cultural differences, through his music specialism.

I still adopted a very western musicological approach, even though I was in China. I didn't really have a very clear view about cultural differences. It didn't occur to me that these people might not even be trying to do the same thing as me.

I assumed that their aesthetic would be the same as mine. So if an instrument sounded odd, I just took it that it was because it was odd; I didn't see that it was because they were trying to do something different.

Thinking for the global market

The case for acquiring foreign languages for the global market is gaining in strength. True, you can get by now without them. But in time, those without the ability to use several languages, even at a fairly superficial level, will disadvantage themselves. There are growing numbers of people with excellent English plus other languages, for employers no longer to need to persist with the exclusive first-language English model.

Beyond languages, there is much valuable experience you can gain from seeking opportunities to work with people from different cultural backgrounds.

- Visit the Virtual Language Library on the Web. This is a high-brow directory that lists databases where information on foreign language web pages and newsgroups is stored. It offers tutorials and language lessons and lists foreign language sites, with more than eighty languages to choose from.
- Plan for cross-cultural experience, e.g. by volunteering to meet and socialize with any foreign delegations visiting your organization.
- Read widely from non-UK sources, like newspapers and magazines.
- Listen to foreign radio stations and watch foreign stations on satellite TV.
- Join networks established specifically to encourage social contact between people of different nationalities.
- Make the most of your existing foreign friends and acquaintances – visit them and telephone them more often.
- Take part in an immersion language course abroad. There is no faster way of getting to know a language and culture than by having to rely entirely on your communication in that language.

Lonesome roads: Learning to work autonomously

Paradoxically in view of our discussion on working in cross-cultural teams, another critical component for a successful global career is the ability to work autonomously.

Although information and communication technology has developed to enable people to stay in contact more readily and fully than a decade ago, local conditions and the effects of the downsizing of organizations often place the travelling or remote employee in a situation where he or she is having to take decisions without being able to refer back or talk through the issues with a line manager or other colleague.

Rory McMahon, who operates across eastern Europe, stresses the need for empowerment as:

> You never know what's round the next corner and you have to make the best of the situation and get the best business you can. Mobile phones don't work very well in eastern Europe. So you need a boss who can trust you enough not to insist on hearing from you for a week at a stretch.
>
> When I'm travelling I have a computer and a modem so I can fax and receive faxes. To be honest, when I'm travelling to eastern Europe, I don't take my laptop if I'm only away for a week in case it gets stolen and I lose all the information. It would be absolute hell if it did. It's backed up, but it would still be a lot of effort. And if it fell into the wrong hands, there would be a lot of difficulty about confidentiality.

McMahon also understands the implications for managing company politics. He's aware how a global employee can be cut off from the organization and lose ground in their career development as a result.

> That's a very real issue and I think before you take a job on you should consider how that position is perceived within the company. Is it thought of as being an upward step? And think about who your communication is going to be through. Will it be direct to management, which is probably the best way to really promote yourself, or is it through a third party who is filtering out the information and then taking credit for your work?

Global survival skills

An important aspect of preparing for a career that crosses national boundaries is the business of survival. You need to feel secure in your surroundings and to gain a sense of belonging to the community in which you live. Some people acclimatize to new environments more readily than others. But it's possible to prepare for the experience, as much through developing an appropriate attitude of mind as by making practical preparations for when the time comes that you need to move.

An important first step is to make yourself aware of the nature of the challenge, and especially the reasons why working outside your home country can turn out to be an unhappy experience.

Eunice Okorocha's research among international students at the University of Surrey identifies among the causes of stress:

- culture shock
- status shock
- loneliness
- homesickness
- getting used to unfamiliar styles of communication.

When Rachel Tyson moved to France she ran up large telephone bills because she missed her friends in the UK. She now feels a very different person, and has outgrown some of her former friends because they don't understand her new way of life. She now enjoys new friendships in France.

Graham Whitehead of British Telecommunications became "quite good at ordering two beers and a cup of white coffee" in his "matey-type French". But when his daughter had appendicitis and was rushed into hospital in France he found himself in difficulty. "I had to start declining verbs because time mattered. After four days of this I did manage to work out the French for 'Excuse me, but I think the intravenous drip is now finished and requires replenishment'. It was only when they realized how appalling my French was that they tried their English, which was equally appalling, so we started drawing pictures and pointing."

Denise Lincoln emphasizes the importance of investing in relationships outside work. "You feel guilty about doing your work; you feel guilty because you're away from your family. If you're not careful and well invested in your relationships, it can be inordinately stressful. Some people just won't do it. I think that's good."

Louis-Dominique Bouzy, currently studying at INSEAD, believes it's important if you go abroad to make the decision jointly with your partner, as integrating with the local community can be more difficult for your partner and children than it is for the person working.

Jonathan Bratt, global account director at A.C. Nielsen, agrees that it needs to be discussed with a partner at an early stage. "So that if the time comes you've discussed it and are prepared for it, rather than saying, 'Oh, by the way I'm going abroad for six months. Is that alright?' It's all part of the preparation."

When he first started working in eastern Europe, Rory McMahon didn't find the marketing part of his job a particular challenge. He was well used to the disciplines involved, from the work he had done inside the UK.

And his anticipation of problems which might arise with respect to the criminal world in Russia didn't materialize.

> OK, you have concerns about the local mafia, the local crime, the potential for being mugged on the trains. You have to go by train everywhere because the planes are a bigger risk from the point of view of them falling out of the sky.
>
> So you adjust. You don't wear as smart a suit as you would in the UK. You try to look more like the locals. Although to be truthful you really do stand out: your dress, your style, your looks, the way you hold your head even is very different from the Russians. Even the way you make eye contact. They just don't do it. You wear sunglasses – you have to buy a new pair of sunglasses to look Russian.
>
> But then my distributor said that my customers liked seeing me dressed as a westerner. So I took the decision to revert to western style, but just keep an eye over my shoulder all the time. And I think it's worked.

Nuclear fall-out was a new challenge for McMahon. "I didn't realize the places I was going to were in the fall-out zone until I left. The distributor I was meeting there was selective about the information he gave me."

Homesickness was the worst problem for Susanna Wong when she first moved from Hong Kong to France. She is very close to her family and worries about how they are. Some of the house-keeping chores caused her to feel out of control too.

It took me a whole day just to apply for a phone line. I went from the company back to home, back to my landlord several times just to make sure I could have the line. In Hong Kong you just need one phone call and that's it.

And when you go to the *préfecture* and you can't really understand what they want and they give you some instructions, you think you understand, and next day you come back and then you go again and you have to give them something else. So you feel lost a lot of the time.

Alexander Rink, who has experienced moving from Canada to work in several European countries, advises people to cultivate their independence, but also to talk to people who have gone through similar experiences. Although he felt very self-confident himself, he found his first year in Portugal an emotional strain. "I don't think I will ever face that kind of difficulty again, because once you've gone through it you cope better."

Jonathan Stock remembered some awkward situations in China when he had a minder from the foreign students' office, "whose job was pretty much to stop us doing anything. It got so bad that we thought of dropping flower pots on her head, by accident of course. Maybe I was a bit too good at doing as I was told, when I should really have smiled nicely but just not bothered about the red tape."

When I interviewed Bridget Jackson, international product manager, I found she had a remarkable facility for mimicking almost every accent she heard. She apologized (not that she needed to) for copying mine. It also helped to account for the ease with which she acclimatized to living in Japan.

I naturally tend to assimilate cultures around me. I seem to adapt quickly to language, to accents or to behavioural patterns and, using the jargon, I tend to "abscond" quickly.

In Japan, I lodged in a homestay with a family. The main difficulty was being able to "break in" to the community. You feel very much like an outsider because although you're absorbing the culture, you are seen as somebody temporary, and so they don't really take much interest in you. But the family I was staying with in Japan were fantastic and were a huge help in making me feel comfortable. The initial difficulty was being accepted.

For two months, outside my job nobody really spoke to me until I met a Japanese girl with whom I struck up a friendship. Through her I was able to access things within the culture that normally a foreigner wouldn't see. I went to all of the ceremonies at new year with her family and went up to the mountain to ring temple bells. Wherever she went, I went with her.

To be honest, I was too busy learning about the culture to feel lonely. But I think part of not wanting to uproot myself now is that I realize how difficult a process it is.

Psychologically, distance has become irrelevant. I'll pick up the phone to friends in Australia or Tokyo, as if they were in the same city. Or if tonight somebody came in and invited me to spend a few days in Egypt, for example, I wouldn't think twice about it, providing I had the time free, of course. So there's a lot more flexibility and adaptability in my behaviour.

My parents never know which country I'm in. But at the bottom of it all I've known that I've had my family's support. I think this was a significant factor, better enabling me to face the difficulties of cultural diversity.

Per Pundsnes, international insurance consultant, sees relationships as the biggest problem for people with global careers.

I've seen very good partnerships break up because they were so far apart for so many years. And that's tough on people who feel they've chosen a job where they can't say "no" to an offer of going to another country.

I've been able to keep in very good contact with friends in Norway. I have to realize that I'm the one who's moving away, and if I want to keep a good close relationship with these people, then I need to be the one who's active all the time.

With some of my very good friends, I can't remember who they're with, or whether they've broken off or where they're up to. It can be awkward and it's a bit worrying. For example when I can't remember what their children are called.

Tripping off the tongue: Jacquie Brighouse, Ruth Knight, Monique Manton and Susan Welford

Jacquie Brighouse, Ruth Knight, Monique Manton and Susan Welford studied languages in England. All four sought experience abroad and were placed in countries in the former Soviet Union, including Russia itself. The mafia, marauders and muggings were among the experiences they witnessed.

Ruth Knight went to Moscow. The first thing that struck her was that it was so dirty. "And it's such a shame because it could be such a beautiful city. You just walk around and you constantly feel something's going to happen to you. It's probably all the media hype because the mafia aren't really interested in students."

She later went to St Petersburg where she found the Russian attitude one of surprise that English people actually wanted to speak Russian. "They were impressed that we were actually making an effort."

Jacquie Brighouse went to Lithuania. She started off being very sceptical. She and three other students "didn't know much about the country, culture or anything. We were all thinking that we would have preferred to go to Moscow. We thought it was going to be dreadful. We'd heard there was still rationing. We were told we would get mugged all the time."

As they were driven from Vilnius airport to the hotel, Brighouse thought, "There are so many nice trees here. So I wasn't depressed like I thought I would be."

Things got even better once they made contact.

> The teachers came round the next day and straight away everyone was lovely to us. We made so many friends. We stayed with a local family. They were just the nicest people. They always used to say to us, "Why are you here studying Russian? This is Lithuania. We speak Lithuanian here." So we started learning some Lithuanian as well: we thought it was a bit rude just going there and speaking Russian all the time.

Later Brighouse went to Moscow. "That was really badly organized. The lessons were poor. We didn't learn anything." These students' home university has since stopped using the Moscow college they went to.

Brighouse recalls that the mafia had contacts in their hostel.

> People had been murdered there. One of our friends
> woke up in the night. There was a roof which you could
> see from the kitchen window. Someone landed on that
> on his back and was twitching and stuff and then died.
> Then there was a Russian girl thrown from the eleventh-
> floor window and her stomach had been cut all open, and
> of course in Moscow then there was snow. They moved
> the body but the blood just stayed for weeks and weeks.

The food they could buy was limited: potatoes, carrots and
onions mainly, unless they went to the western shops with their
very high prices. "You couldn't really get any nice meat. My
parents sent me food parcels every week."

Susan Welford enjoyed living in Moscow. "It's such a big place
and there are so many things to visit. You meet so many different
people – it's really good."

She resolutely wants to go back, even though life was hard. She
laughs off the danger too. "You just have to keep your wits about
you and know the areas where you shouldn't go on your own."

Monique Manton stayed at a student hostel in Moscow. She
found the biggest problem was the cold. The lectures were excellent, though.

> One of the lecturers was really sweet – a bit dippy. She
> kept telling us to eat rice and carrots: "Everything else
> is bad for you", she told us. No alcohol. No coffee. No
> tea. No chocolate. When she caught us eating a Mars
> bar, she'd call us *hooliganki*, because she thought we
> shouldn't be eating chocolate – it was bad for us and
> we'd get fat. She was really concerned for us.

All the students felt they had become a lot more independent
as a result of the experience. Manton comments, "I feel I can do
anything, go anywhere. Nothing in travelling will faze me."

The assorted experiences of these students underlines the need
for students wanting to study abroad to plan thoroughly and take
appropriate precautions.

- Make sure your university has two or three of you going to the
  same location. A group of students can cope with problems in
  a situation where one alone might go under.
- Get your accommodation sorted out before you arrive.
- Talk to somebody who's already been to your destination. You
  need to know what to expect.

- Make contact with the locals as quickly as possible; don't let opportunities go by.
- Find out where the dangerous areas are and don't go out alone.
- Persevere. You can put up with an enormous amount, as long as you know that you're acquiring skills that amount to a priceless investment in your career.

Companies that send employees abroad often take considerable care over supporting them in finding accommodation, getting a driving licence, seeing to health needs, insurance and so on. But more often this service is provided only for those working for long periods overseas. One of the consequences of downsizing is that those who have to travel for short periods are left making their own arrangements. Small businesses which operate internationally also tend to leave it up to their nomads to make their own arrangements.

There are contrasting values that Denise Lincoln will never get used to. "It's shocking to go to Vietnam and see beautiful three-year-old children sent into the nightclubs to beg. You know you can't win because if you don't give them money they get beaten and if you do give them money it will just exacerbate that way of life."

All these elements strengthen the case for thorough long-term preparation for a global career, even extending to such mundane matters as personal hygiene. Action that might involve a low risk in Europe or North America can have serious consequences elsewhere. Attitudes to sexual behaviour, for example, need to be established and then self-discipline adhered to, given the nature of the risks.

Thinking for the global market

If you conclude that you need to lay the foundations for the challenge of the global market by being equipped to work outside the UK, then now is the time to begin your preparation. As with so many other elements of this book, it is the mental preparation that is crucial to successful outcomes.

We can't, of course, address all the dimensions which will give rise to a successful career in a particular country that you might have your eye on. There are specialist books on the subject of individual countries which you will want to refer to if you intend to spend time in a particular country. What we're addressing here is more general preparation: we have seen that the career of a global nomad isn't necessarily one that involves long stints abroad.

It's the ability to communicate globally that's more important than setting up one's base in a particular country. This is not an exploration, then, aimed to prepare the budding expatriate for a five-year stint in Morocco or Malaysia.

You can be a global nomad with a permanent base in the UK, as long as you're able to travel to and communicate with the places you need to be in touch with in order to meet the needs of your employer, the requirements of your own business, or the particular contracts you are fulfilling at any one point in your career.

Activity for the global market: Platform for a nomadic quest

In chapter 4 we examined the extent to which you might be ready to pursue a career in the global market. Let's now take up some of those themes and pursue the sorts of action you need to be confident with in order to make the global grade.

We need to consider two dimensions:

• your personal and professional circumstances
• your acclimatization to the requirements of global communication.

For each of these dimensions you need to reflect upon:

• your current situation
• future developments which might affect your situation
• what action you can take to achieve a predisposition to mobility.

Let's pursue these in more depth.

Your personal and professional circumstances

Start by writing, below, those circumstances which you feel will enable you to move freely outside the UK. Then log the inhibitors that are likely to prevent you. You will see some examples, but these are not exhaustive and might not apply to you in any event.

For example, having children is usually thought of as an inhibitor to mobility, especially as many parents believe that their children need a stable educational environment. However, growing numbers of parents take responsibility themselves for educating their children. So for them it doesn't matter how many times they move as they're not tied to a specific educational institution.

Another variation might apply to parents with different first languages who bring up their children to be bilingual. It's often the case that both parents welcome the opportunity to allow their children to live in both parents' home countries.

The examples below, then, are only intended to be illustrative, and will not apply in all circumstances.

Personal and professional circumstances favouring global mobility might be:

- being single
- having a partner but no children
- being self-employed in the knowledge sector
- being employed by a multinational company
- having considerable investments abroad
- having friends and relatives abroad.

Personal and professional circumstances that might inhibit global mobility are:

- having significant caring responsibilities
- being in debt
- owning a business with a large local clientele
- having worked in a single company for a long time
- having a partner whose own career demands are incompatible with a global career.

There are many possible examples, of course. Take stock of your own personal circumstances and list those elements which favour your mobility in the left-hand column of the table below and, in the right-hand column, those which might inhibit it.

YOUR CURRENT PERSONAL AND PROFESSIONAL CIRCUMSTANCES

Current mobility enhancers	Current mobility inhibitors
•	•
•	•
•	•
•	•
•	•
•	•

Next consider those factors that you already know about, both personal and professional, which could affect your potential mobility either way over the next three years or so: i.e. either increasing it or reducing it. Any of the examples we looked at above could be relevant here, or there could be new factors, such as children leaving home. List those factors which will increase your potential mobility in the left column, and the potential restraints on your mobility in the right.

YOUR FUTURE PERSONAL AND PROFESSIONAL CIRCUMSTANCES

Future mobility enhancers   Future mobility inhibitors
•   •
•   •
•   •
•   •
•   •
•   •

Your acclimatization to the requirements of global communication

Now assess the extent to which you're able to communicate effectively with people of non-UK background. Remember that our understanding of global mobility (and hence communication) is a wide one, including communication via the Internet or by telephone.

You will remember that we looked at this dimension in chapter 4, but in that chapter we set out some specific parameters, whereas now the only limit is set by your own imagination. The examples below will show the breadth of context that we're encouraging in this part of the activity.

Examples of dimensions of global communication are:

• ability to use foreign languages
• experience of working successfully in multicultural teams
• frequent communication with people in other countries by letter, telephone, fax, videoconferencing or via the Internet
• sensitivity to the different norms and expectations of specific cultures
• regular reading of non-UK newspapers and magazines

- having a CV or portfolio which meets the requirements and expectations of companies in one or more countries
- knowledge of how to obtain accommodation in particular countries
- knowledge of other countries' taxation systems.

In the next segment of this activity, then, take stock of those elements of global communication you are well prepared for and those elements which both are relevant to you and are among your weak spots.

YOUR ACCLIMATIZATION TO THE REQUIREMENTS OF GLOBAL COMMUNICATION

Global communication: areas of strength	Global communication: areas of weakness
•	•
•	•
•	•
•	•
•	•
•	•

What action you can take to achieve a predisposition to global mobility?

Finally, set out for both dimensions of:

- your personal and professional circumstances
- your global communication skills and experience

those areas you consider you can change or develop, and how you propose to pursue that development.

YOUR GLOBAL MOBILITY

Areas for development and change	Action to be pursued
•	•
•	•
•	•
•	•
•	•
•	•

Thinking for the global market

The remarkable advances in communication technology, allied with the inherent unpleasantness of a lifestyle which involves a lot of travel, will result in there being more communication and less travel in proportion to the total volume of business in the global economy.

There will be occasions, of course, where human contact will be indispensable because you will need to experience the body language, shake hands, smell the pheromones and drink the champagne. On those occasions, the hours you spend on the plane to and from your destination, and the days you spend recovering from jet lag afterwards, will be calculated to be a worthwhile sacrifice.

But communication technology will remove the need for much of that nasty travelling by enabling us to make more meaningful visual contact over large distances. (I should acknowledge that some people actually like travelling.)

For the global careerist, that places a greater emphasis than ever on the ability to communicate. In the longer term, communicating across language and cultural differences will be the fundamental talent that takes precedence over all other skills. The global economy is an environment in which great communicators flourish.

Hence the importance of acquiring foreign languages, though you can get by without them. It's also why I have emphasized cross-cultural understanding, which is very definitely not optional.

Among the other global career investments we have examined in this chapter, you will have logged the following as sources of immense advantage:

- Research the formats of CVs (as that's what they're still called) that are standard in the countries you might want to work in.
- Record all your international experience to date and seek to maximize it.
- Build up your networks of non-UK business contacts.
- Take every opportunity you can to host non-UK delegations to your organization.
- Cultivate an international personal and business image – brand yourself as the most natural person to choose for interaction with people from other countries and representing different cultures.

Finally, even if you don't rate your own foreign language ability, remember that there are characteristics unrelated to language competence which you need to develop in order to be successful in a global business environment. The essential ones are:

- *Genuine communication*: the ability to share meaningful discussion in preference to lecturing people with different or opposed cultural expectations.
- *Empathy*: the ability to see a situation from the other person's perspective.
- *Respect for those from different cultural backgrounds*: showing appreciation for alternative perspectives.
- *Integration of task and relationship elements of a work project*: learning to be person oriented as well as task oriented.
- *Tolerance of ambiguity*: the ability to live and work comfortably in unfamiliar and unpredictable cross-cultural contexts.
- *Persistence*: the ability to continue to work towards your targets despite setbacks.
- *Flexibility*: recognition that there is more than one way to reach a goal.

The Digital Portfolio: Career Strategies Beyond the Lifetime Career

All the world's a soap ...

The future doesn't have to consist of the toxic half-life that the more melancholy members of the future-of-work Opinionate offer us. A long-term career strategy, constantly updated, can give rise to security and fulfilment in the global market. In the coming years the focus of our career strategies will be a combination of text, images and sounds that form the package that succeeds the CV: the digital portfolio.

To be sure, we will be able to trace the progression from the current CV in all its multifarious forms to the digital portfolio. I am not suggesting that the transformation will happen overnight. And the content of the digital portfolio will include many of the typical features of the paper-based CV, such as:

- personal details
- qualifications
- employment history
- achievements
- skills
- interests.

I shall argue that it won't only be the format, texture, maintenance and transmission properties of the digital portfolio which will be different from the traditional CV. More important, the activity associated with its design and execution will be of a different order from what typically is invested into today's CVs.

The essential difference is between passive and retrospective compilation of a selection of materials, and application of focused endeavour which generates a creative interaction between career-oriented activity and its encapsulation in digital form.

The global careerist will invest into the digital portfolio the constant craft and attention that TV producers lavish on demate-rialized global products like *Neighbours* and *Coronation Street*. Putting together this living dossier will demand more creative endeavour than the mechanical recording of past events.

You will need to generate the kind of experience that will create a magnetic, new-style portfolio. Arranging your portfolio will be as challenging as writing a screenplay, sharpening your imagination and engaging your skills in planning and negotiation. Your pursuit of quality material to put in the portfolio won't leave you short of cliff hangers.

In this chapter we explore an integrated strategy which antici-pates shifts in recruitment practice, organizational demand and advances in IT, to produce the design for a digital portfolio aimed at maximizing and maintaining prospects for a lifetime of income generation through work contracts.

In particular we examine:

- how to approach choices about self-investment in skills and professional or vocational expertise, and especially how early you should begin to specialize
- the successor to the traditional CV, the digital portfolio, and how to manage it
- the generic skills you need to develop in addition to your specialist expertise and abilities
- how to create a safety net for yourself as a hedge against uncer-tainty.

Trading in assets

There is one calculated risk we each take during our lives that has more far-reaching consequences than any other – even our choice of partner. This is the professional or vocational skills and expertise we choose to pursue.

I have just implied that this choice is a one-off. But in reality it comes as a series of decision points, subject to constant revision or adaptation and, increasingly, change of direction. The amalgam of all these decisions can result in you investing years acquiring the knowledge and skills to support a particular vocation or profession, only to find them going through the shredder as technology or new organizational forms make them obsolete.

So how do you decide which particular occupational area to pursue? Are the chances of finding a spectrum of expertise which will maintain its long-term value as random as a spread bet on how long the monarchy will remain a job for life? And once you have chosen your occupational area, are you in for further uncertainty as you select specific knowledge and skills to develop within that area?

Take the example of IT as an occupational area. For those embarking on a career in computing, choosing where to start can be very complicated. There is certainly a demand for computer skills; every organization of any size needs computing expertise.

But the role has changed in recent years. Whereas in the 1980s those employed in computer departments of large organizations were usually programmers and systems analysts, today they're more likely to be consultants providing advice and training for other managers and staff, maintaining local area networks and linking them with global telecommunications networks.

Career progression in the industry tends to move from trainee programmer to designer of new systems, systems analyst and subsequently project leader. From then on, senior jobs are involved in the management of the business.

Some get into the industry with degrees in computer science, or higher national qualifications from the Business and Technology Education Council or the Scottish Vocational Education Council. Others have degrees which include some computing, without making them a specialist in any particular area. Many of those who have graduated in an unrelated subject have pursued postgraduate conversion courses into IT.

IT is a fast-moving area, and many more occupational areas will accelerate to the pace of change experienced in computing. So IT provides a useful testbed from which to infer the kind of strategy to adopt in other occupational areas subject to accelerating change.

The questions arising from the IT experience are:

• Do you base your self-investment on your hunches about how the market will develop?
• Or do you try to keep your options open, investing in your generic skills for as long as possible, and commit yourself to a specific vocational area as late as you dare?

Even the evidence of IT, a highly specialized and technical occupational area, illustrates the advantages of the second of these alternatives. Training for IT in the 1980s failed to anticipate the short-term currency of programming skills and left many in the industry needing to retrain and develop a broader understanding of the nature and needs of the organizations they worked for. Those with the necessary flexibility and determination to acquire new knowledge adapted successfully.

Can the experience of IT-based occupations be extrapolated to other occupational areas? One can't apply the IT model crudely of course, but the fact that IT has helped to bring about changes in so many organizations outside the actual discipline of IT does indicate some significant pointers.

Just as the technology of mass production led to the assembly line and its management hierarchy, so has IT given rise to the adoption of flexible working practices within holistic companies. These organizations require employees who have the ability to see a process through from start to finish, rather than specializing in a narrow range of tasks at a particular point in the production or service cycle.

This redeployment of human resources has come about because there are increasing synergies between tasks, as a consequence of what computers can do. It's now easier for one person to see to all the needs of a customer, from taking an order and arranging delivery, to sending out the bill and dealing with problems, than to have separate departments contributing to a giant organizational conveyor belt. It's the same for a factory worker completing the cycle from operation of robotic machinery to improving product design.

This means that the balance of advantage is clearly with the generalist who keeps their options open, rather than the premature specialist. Holistic companies need employees who are articulate, have a broad understanding of the company's mission and purposes, are versatile and can respond creatively, speedily and flexibly to problems that arise.

Thus investment in an updated, broad-based, liberal education, which encourages an ability to switch between tasks with ease, provides a surer foundation than an approach which tries to anticipate movements in the skills market for years and decades in advance.

This means that there must be an element within each individual's strategy, to counterbalance the encouragement within the

UK education and training system to specialize early. Keep your
options open. And when you do go down a particular professional or vocational route, continue to invest in generic skills and
abilities. We shall return to the nature of these generic skills later
in this chapter.

Unnatural selection

The traditional CV belongs to yesterday. Its ability to secure a
contract of any value for an individual in the global labour market
is dissipating because it is:

- one-dimensional: a flat, text-based archive which gives little idea
  of what the person can achieve in an organizational setting
- static, and subject only to spasmodic updating
- generalized, rather than tailored to the specific expectations of
  individual companies
- the outcome of experience, rather than the driving force behind
  it.

Increasingly companies are recruiting through new communications media. Recruitment and selection systems are available on
CD-ROM and via the Internet. Many companies see the use of
these media as contributing to the techno-smart image that they
want to project. They're also handy for screening out those who
are not computer literate or who are unable to take advantage of
the new media.

The advantage of a digital recruitment database to employers
is that they can input specific search parameters and have an
instant print-out of the potential applicants who meet their
criteria. From the point of view of the applicant, the more search
fields your name appears in, the greater your chances become
of attracting potential employers. Don't expect the phone to
start ringing if all you have is a degree in Sanskrit – or even in
engineering if you have nothing else to support it.

One illustration of selection by database is *The European* newspaper's international skills database. Its aim is to help companies
search more effectively for the job seekers who best meet their
needs. The database contains summaries of highly skilled international job hunters and is updated daily.

The European's database provides profiles of thousands of
people seeking high-level jobs in every sector of commerce. It

saves employers the trouble of reading through thousands of paper CVs, by sorting the data into specified search fields.

The database is also a harbinger of the intensity of the competition for work contracts that we will experience in the global market. The people who advertise their skills in *The European* are multilingual, mobile, highly educated and with a wide range of professional skills and experience.

A more visually rich version of the career profiles database is provided by recruitment agency MacTemps, which offers employers an interactive CD-ROM carrying a selection of its candidates' portfolios. The programme is designed to allow companies to judge an applicant's work on screen, before setting up an interview. It's another illustration of how new technology is making the traditional CV obsolete.

The concept of the internal profile, which employees maintain for the companies which they already work for, is also growing. We have already seen how, for example, the multinational computer software company Logica insists that its own staff keep their personal profiles up to date as part of their normal working routine. Each individual's experience and competences are then assessed as new project teams are put together.

The company also insists that staff profiles are written to a common format. The Logica approach illustrates how the discipline of continuously recording one's skills and experience will become a prerequisite for getting work within the company which employs you – let alone for trying to find a new employer.

Another example is the intranet set up by the BBC, with the purpose of enabling its technicians to put their CVs on-line. Using an intranet with video and sound capabilities enables these camera operatives to show excerpts from their work, along with the traditional information on a CV. This gives them the opportunity to show off their best output.

Many companies are setting up huge global databases of people to offer to employers. The software identifies detailed fits against customized criteria. Employers will take advantage to get just the person they need. Although qualifications will be the starting point, everyone will need to accumulate experience that constitutes their own individual unique selling point.

The battle is on for the killer package in recruitment database design which captures the world market, in the way that Microsoft Windows has done in the operating system market. Once the winner has emerged from the pile, we will all be producing portfolios matched to the parameters of the dominant first-stage recruitment software package.

The digital portfolio

We're still in the early stages of the movement towards continent-wide and global recruitment and selection. But our strategies for lifetime employment must anticipate where technology and business priorities are taking us. We need to examine what will happen to recruitment processes over the next decade, to enable us to develop appropriate responses in good time for the arrival of global digital selection.

This is not to say that the face-to-face interview will be replaced by electronic methods of search and selection. There will still be selection by interview, although, as we saw in chapter 2, that interview is increasingly likely to occur at a distance, using video-conferencing technology. Nevertheless, it will be electronic methods that will be applied to drawing up shortlists, so that a design fault in your portfolio will result in your never getting past that critical initial filter.

Electronic Résumé Revolution by Joyce Kennedy and Thomas Morrow describes how organizations using scanning technology and automated tracking systems have improved the effectiveness of their recruitment processes. It explains how the most sophisticated automated applicant tracking systems extract and summarize key applicant data such as skills, employment history and qualifications. These systems then evaluate this data against current and future vacancies, flagging matches to the recruiter.

The book suggests ways of writing computer-friendly CVs, e.g. using keyword summaries. It also provides advice on how to organize information for agency CV databases. Kennedy and Morrow argue that simple fonts, plenty of buzz words and avoiding too many graphics are the most effective ways of getting your CV noticed by computer.

However, while this text-based approach is acceptable for the present, it will not meet the requirements of the contract seekers of the future. Chris Brewster, director of the Centre for European Human Resource Management at Cranfield University, agrees that the technology for the digital portfolio is available and is set to replicate throughout business organizations in the years to come.

"I think that as the more computer literate generation comes through, people are going to accept that more and more."

The days of the static CV are numbered. We need to think in terms of rolling portfolios: multimedia productions that change from one week to the next as you record and illustrate the latest work you have completed or log in a recent updating to your skills.

It will no longer be a document that you revise once every couple of years or when you start applying for a new job. The work you did a year or six months ago will lose its attraction to employers (including your current one if, like an increasing number of companies, they require you to keep an up-to-date portfolio), because their business has moved on and technology has developed. Consequently, the importance of continuously updating your portfolio will become critical to your career.

We can expect to use software that facilitates updating of portfolios at frequent intervals, and for that information to be transmitted automatically to amend the files that we have forwarded to potential employers or recruitment agencies.

The recruitment process will be subject to more radical change. At the moment, looking for a new job involves an act of will and a disruption to our normal routine, as we assess our qualifications and experience and revise our CVs as a part of our self-promotion. Once we have the on-line digital portfolio, movement between jobs and contracts will be more fluid and more frequent.

Our portfolios will be scanned daily by employers who are looking for a match. Offers of jobs and contracts will come regularly to those with recent experience which the employer finds enticing. Our working lives will no longer consist of periods of steady-state employment, punctuated only occasionally by a round of job applications.

Instead, we will expect to receive project and contract offers on the strength of the digital portfolio that we have made available to the relevant recruitment networks. This process will accelerate as more people undertake work on the polycontractual basis that we examined in chapter 2.

A greater proportion of our time will be spent on securing contracts and keeping in work. Those seeking contracts from several employers simultaneously will constantly be applying the principles of marketing to their efforts. That will require, in addition to ensuring continuous currency for their digital portfolios, keeping up to date with new technology and training and ensuring that they network widely.

Track records

The digital portfolio opens up all manner of opportunities to employers to examine the credentials of job and contract applicants. Hitherto employers have had to work from within the limitations of narratives of previous experience together with degrees, professional and vocational certificates and the infrastructure of skills and knowledge accreditation.

This information has only been useful as a general filter for weeding out clearly inappropriate applicants. However, the panoply of selection processes used to single out a winner from several shortlisted candidates for a particular job still leaves too much to chance. There's no one involved in recruitment and selection who doesn't have a rich repertoire of stories to recount about the disastrous appointments they (or more usually their colleagues) have made.

No one has yet found a consistent and reliable solution to this problem. Granted, you can reduce the odds by using external consultants, by putting candidates through a variety of assessment exercises and so on. But one of the biggest weaknesses in recruitment and selection is that initial filter, where the majority of candidates are discarded on the basis of the written evidence they have produced.

This gives rise to the instant knock-out phenomenon: the immediate recognition by the recruiter conducting an interview that the candidate she or he is talking to just doesn't fit the organization or the team they would be allocated to. The complementary problem is less often recognized but has consequences that are as serious. This is the potential excellent-fit candidate who hasn't been invited to the final selection process because he or she has fallen at the initial sifting.

By contrast, a digital portfolio which, for example, shows clips of the candidate involved in team work or leadership activity, will provide much clearer evidence, at the pre-interview stage, of the extent to which the candidate will fit the organization. This will result in the compilation of more targeted shortlists and the achievement of better geared appointments.

Many employers bemoan the failure of the education system to produce people with business-related skills like leadership and initiative. The problem here is that these abilities are not measurable other than within specific contexts. How can employers know what they're really getting when talents like leadership and attitudes such as flexibility, enthusiasm and initiative – the employ-ability skills that industrialists so often draw attention to – are contingent upon the environment in which the person works?

Writers on organizations from Machiavelli to Mintzberg have been searching for generalizations that underpin behaviour in organizations. In the end they have concluded that most of the outcomes they describe are contingent upon circumstances. And that's the problem: it all depends.

Similarly attempts to find ways of accrediting business-related skills and attitudes have failed. The fact that you provide effective leadership in one organization doesn't mean that, even if you were to use exactly the same approach in another, your leader-ship would be just as effective. Ask any manager of a premiership football team.

This uncertainty will prompt an increasing demand from employers to individual applicants to provide evidence in multi-media form of their skills being used in business contexts. Advances in IT now offer systems that will give employers more focused evidence of whether your style will fit the culture and values that currently characterize their organization.

That's not to say that the multimedia digital portfolio will take the place of assessment exercises, psychometric tests and so on. But we can expect a growing demand for digital portfolios to be submitted in order to ensure more effective initial filtering of applicants, with employers setting out their parameters and indi-viduals compiling evidence that provides a good fit from a wider and growing range of material they have about themselves.

Screen play

The sequel to the CV, then, won't be a printed representation of our potential value to an employer. It will be an amalgam of text, sound, and still and moving images which will bring to life what we are, as much as what we've done. We will constantly find ways to enhance it.

We might want to include clips or soundbites to illustrate how we:

- run a meeting
- negotiate on the telephone
- deal with a complaint from a customer

- work with a team on a new design
- act in a play
- give a speech at a wedding dinner.

Or it might provide evidence of a host of other contexts that will show a potential employer, more effectively than the current CV can, the spectrum of skills, attitudes and personality traits that will be at the company's disposal.

This new-style profile will give a variety of illustrations of our paid work or, especially for those who haven't secured a first contract yet, work experience achievements, voluntary work outputs, accomplishments at school or college, or any other evidence which will demonstrate potential value to an employer.

As scanners, camcorders, image editing software and the stream of digital information storage, presentation and transmission devices become cheaper and pass into everyday use, we will be constantly on the look-out for opportunities to provide footage, soundtrack, text, rendering, design work etc., to incorporate into our digital portfolios. These will be published on the Internet, with links wherever possible to our other achievements or publications stored on other servers.

As the search engines used by employers to sift through masses of data produced by ever-growing numbers of contract seekers worldwide become increasingly sophisticated in what they can select and reject, so will we have to keep finding new angles from which to present ourselves, to maximize our chances of meeting the employer's minimum search parameters.

The very existence of these search engines will also require intelligent and imaginative organization and presentation of portfolio materials. Although not everyone will be able to afford to buy consultancy support, the digital portfolio will have to look polished. Portfolios that display digital and visual illiteracy or the production values of a home video will be tomorrow's equivalent of today's misspelt and ungrammatical letter of application.

The digital portfolio will have the information arranged thematically. For example, if you want to demonstrate to prospective employers that you have the qualities of determination and perseverance, your digital portfolio might include one or more of:

- a certificate stating that you have completed a run in a marathon
- a photograph you have taken of an elusive species of mammal
- a local newspaper report of a community drama production you have put on

- footage of you taking a truckload of medical supplies to Croatia
- a manager's description of how you delivered a contract to deadline despite the odds
- soundtrack of you persuading some colleagues to adopt your proposals for a sales strategy.

If you wanted to show your effectiveness as a team worker, you could present a collection of evidence which might include:

- soundtrack of a workgroup discussion on a sensitive personnel issue, in which you contribute to achieving a consensus on how to deal with it
- footage of you playing rugby or hockey
- graphs showing the sales figures of your team compared with those of others in the company, or your previous year's performance
- an executive summary of a position paper you have produced on an issue you're dealing with as a member of a parent–teacher association
- stills of an exhibition you have organized with a number of colleagues.

The potential list is endless. But each of the digital folios that make up the whole portfolio must be brief, and focused to make a particular point about you. The software designers will provide search targets, which will enable recruiters to pinpoint the areas that interest them. The objective for the editor will be to hit as many targets as possible with high-quality, convincing material.

A single mismatch between your own skills and those the prospective employer is looking for will leave your details hibernating in the database rather than in the printer bin ready for the employer to follow up. Thus the digital portfolio reinforces the argument for developing a broad range of skills as against early specialization. Time invested in displaying positive work attitudes will also pay dividends.

We will see a new consultancy industry extending the range of the current complement of outplacement agencies and career development advisers, which will combine the disciplines of career planning, portfolio design, sound and vision recording, editing and mixing, promotion and packaging.

Thinking for the global market

This is not to say that we will all be followed around by our own personal camera and sound crews. The technology is developing to the extent that it has already become miniaturized and easy to manipulate. It only needs the mass market to take off for prices to tumble. Organizations too will adapt and absorb expectations in relation to the recording of bankable work experience, to be absorbed into individual portfolios.

So the point of this exploration of the nature of the digital portfolio of the future is not to create a nation of gaffers, grips and best boys. Rather it is to stress the importance of the development of generic skills alongside any professional or vocational expertise, in preparation for the demands of the digital portfolio. Global careerists need to make that investment as early as possible and to maintain it throughout their working lives.

It's easy to predict what will happen to the currency of qualifications in the digital portfolio environment. You might have a certificate to show that you know your way round the travel and tourism business. But it will be the on-line material you generate for your portfolio which will show an employer how your customers respond to you or how well you work in a holistic team.

Qualifications will still be one of the preconditions for gaining a contract, but it will be what you include on your digital portfolio that will make the difference between success and failure, or more important in the longer term, in determining whether the contract you negotiate will provide you with the best opportunities to add further commercial value to your digital compilation.

There will be times when you want to kick yourself because you had an outstanding experience which you didn't record or for which there was no witness available to corroborate your achievement. We will need to be ready to capture an experience for inclusion in our portfolios. For customers, too, it will become routine to be asked for permission to have an interaction recorded for assimilation into a digital portfolio.

There will be other consequences too. Ageism is likely to recede even without the legislation to outlaw it. True, there will still be ways for employers to disguise their intentions. If they have a covert policy to employ only those under forty, they won't have to bother to specify that fact in their job advertisements, as the database search engine will automatically exclude anyone who doesn't meet the specified criteria.

On the other hand, it will be just as easy for the search to throw up the candidates who can demonstrate dynamism, team skills, leadership qualities, and other parameters required by the employer, whatever their age. On balance the digital portfolio is more likely to act as a powerful antidote to ageism, as employers have before their eyes the evidence that will challenge prejudice.

As the technology develops to enable us to create a permanent record of any aspect of our lives which we believe will have a commercial value in the global labour market, so will we be constantly aware of how an event or particular strand of experience might look on our digital portfolios.

It will dominate our thinking as we muse, ". . . I wonder how that would look on my portfolio? How could I present it to best advantage?" The standard party-goer's question, "what do you do for a living?" will be replaced by, "what have you logged on your portfolio lately?" Your decisions about what you include, exclude, and discard as out of date, will feature significantly in your success rate for clinching the contracts that most interest you.

Our exploration of the digital portfolio also confirms the conclusion we reached in chapter 5 about the kinds of skills we need to invest in. We suggested there that, although we need to develop expertise in a particular vocational or professional realm, we should delay irrevocable decisions for as long as possible. In addition we need to develop generic skills.

Until now, employers have been able to take on people secure in the knowledge that their certificates vouch for the specific skills and expertise they have. But they have been flying blind in terms of the personal and generic business skills that they've been looking for, relying mainly on psychometric tests and interview performance as the best available, though not especially reliable, measures of the broader spectrum of accomplishments that their organizations are seeking.

The digital portfolio will make a huge difference in cutting down for employers the risk entailed in recruitment and selection. So when we're designing our portfolios, we will need to select their content on the basis of our understanding of what employers are looking for, over and above the knowledge and competences validated through our qualifications and the experience logged in previous jobs.

Despite the inconsistent views generated from employers on this issue, the necessary generic competences are easy to identify. They coincide with the skills that each of us will need if we find ourselves having to secure an income outside an organizational framework. We examine that aspect of portfolio management next.

Home alone

We no longer enjoy the economic certainty enjoyed by those born between the end of the First World War and 1950. Those generations could afford the luxury of choosing almost any career in the knowledge that it would bring a secure – if not spectacular – income for half a century. Now any career can turn into a bunjee jumper's nightmare. Each of us needs a safety net.

The wise strategy is to identify and develop those skills that you would need to become self-employed, because not only do these provide a source of security, they also enable you to convince prospective employers (who are, after all, more interested in their own survival and prosperity than anything else) that you have a broad portfolio of skills that will add value to their business.

Whether or not you accept Handy's arguments about the spread of the portfolio career, having the skills that could take you down the portfolio route serves a dual purpose. Not only are you able to secure the contracts you need for economic survival; you can also ensure a reliable income stream if circumstances conspire against your continuing in organizational employment.

You don't need an MBA to acquire the necessary portfolio skills. The grounding you should be looking for includes:

- IT applications
- financial management
- numerical reasoning
- organizational psychology
- marketing
- market research
- interpersonal skills
- self-starter disciplines
- negotiating skills
- telephone skills.

These are the basic elements you need to make yourself in demand as a contract worker.

Portfolio people have three levels of loyalty:

- the first to their own professional development and career
- the second to their current project, contract, team or assignment
- the third to the organization to which they currently have a contractual commitment.

When you're working for yourself, your digital portfolio will be designed to generate not a single job, but combinations of contracts to be held at the same time. It will be organized not to convince employers that you're worth taking on for the next ten years, but to demonstrate the kind of quality of work you can produce in chunks of say ten or a hundred hours.

Not only is portfolio working intensely motivating: discrete targets, no ambiguity, no office politics and the luxury of organizing your own schedule and your own life; it also encourages you to identify the skills which are necessary to your own survival, to invest in them, and then to convince a contract manager of their value to him.

Thus another reason for developing the breadth of your skills and range of your portfolio is so that you can negotiate from a position of strength with prospective contract managers. Your aim is to get them to add value to your portfolio in the same way as you will add value to their organization. Some elements will be provided automatically because of the very nature of the company, such as the opportunity to participate in multicultural teams if it's a multinational.

As you research the potential companies you might be interested in, draw up your own shortlist of characteristics that you might be looking for, and examine the evidence to see if the company coincides with your desired profile. Such characteristics might include:

- a multicultural corporate environment
- a commitment to individual development
- opportunities to update skills continuously
- experience of foreign cultures and business practices
- willingness of colleagues to socialize
- opportunities to make a contribution to the wider community
- a participative management style.

There's another element to the portfolio strategy that ties into the developments in technology which we have already discussed. This is the ease with which one can now set up in business. The setting up costs for those working in the knowledge industry are small: you don't need more than a computer, modem and printer. In addition, because your potential market is global, you won't need a huge hit rate to generate a reasonable income.

Don't get carried away with this: but there's also the chance of hitting the supercharged business league too. One idea, one star performance, can generate an income to last a lifetime. It's reputation that makes the impact here.

An orchestral conductor who makes a landmark recording, an actor who delivers a stunning performance, a cookery writer, an industrial troubleshooter, a born again communicator – any of these can attract enormous incomes with hardly any additional effort once their reputation has been made. It's their celebrity that causes the demand for the individual to explode. At that point, amount of talent relative to others in the same field doesn't count for much.

The dematerialized economy is spreading this phenomenon. A surgeon, an economist, an acoustics expert, an organizational consultant, can all make use of technology to spread their expertise over a wider market. There are no longer geographical restrictions to trading in the ultimate dematerialized product: the idea.

Activity for the global market: Preparing the groundwork for your digital portfolio

Our activity in this chapter is an exploration of what you can do to prepare yourself for the age of the digital portfolio. This exercise addresses the design stage of the process. You don't need to go out and buy a state of the art camcorder or hire a mixing studio. You're aiming to:

- develop an instinct for generating enticing material to include in your portfolio
- complete the mental preparation to enable you to negotiate effectively to secure the kind of experience that will give rise to high-quality portfolio material.

This is an exercise at the design stage, then. You're preparing yourself for the time when your career profile will be presented in digital format. I'm not suggesting that you create such a product now. The design stage is arguably the most important part of the preparation. The production stage might be more fun, but it's less challenging because it's only a matter of putting together material that is the outcome of your planning and negotiating.

A digital portfolio is one which uses a multimedia framework to market yourself to potential employers and those managing and tendering contracts for specific projects. Think of the product in terms of hierarchical levels of information, with an overarching statement of the offer you're making to those contract managers, with signposts to more detailed subsets of information about yourself and what your offer represents in terms of benefits to that potential client. These signposts will be highlighted so that the reader can click open further information about you.

Here's one example of an opening text, compiled by Mark Richards. His skeleton digital portfolio demonstrates that:

- The whole process is simple and doesn't take any special expertise.
- It's never too early to start recording and compiling relevant experience.
- The very challenge of compiling a digital portfolio makes one look at work and work-related opportunities in a new light, often generating experiences that can be exploited as part of a self-marketing exercise.

Users of the Web will be aware of the convention that underlined text constitutes an access point to a sub-hierarchy of information. So, for example, clicking on the word "*deutsch*" in the opening segment of the portfolio would open a new file with the portfolio set out in German.

The following extract is based on the portfolio of one of the witnesses I interviewed for this book. It illustrates how managing a digital portfolio requires:

- crisply written text
- material that can be presented in several media
- clear architecture to enable readers to navigate around it easily
- constant updating.

In order to work up a template for your own digital portfolio, you will need to compile, in addition to the usual items associated with the traditional CV such as qualifications and employment history, primary source evidence of your skills, relevant to your work context, in the following formats:

- text
- sound

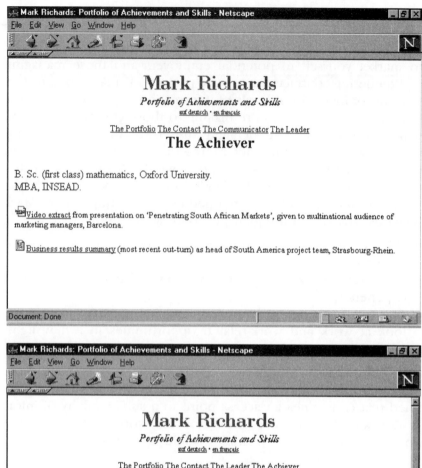

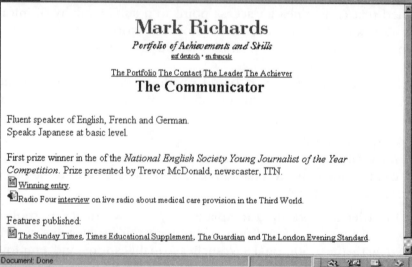

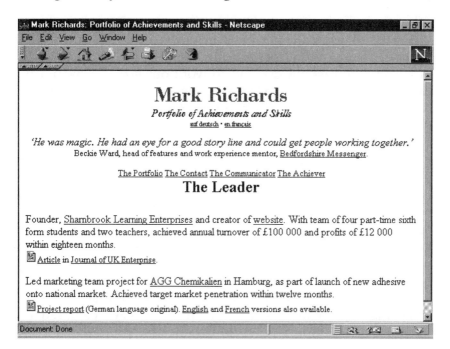

- still picture
- moving picture
- combinations of all the above.

Some of these, especially the moving pictures, might prove difficult in the short term. It's only as videoconferencing and routine video recordings of meetings become the norm, that source material such as this will become readily available for inclusion in individual digital portfolios.

Nevertheless there will still be opportunities which will either arise naturally, or which you will be able to help along. For example there are many courses on presentation skills or on dealing with the media, which routinely record on videotape the performance of participants. Rigorous editing of such material can produce a few seconds of footage that show you as an accomplished communicator.

You could also record your telephone calls for a couple of days, and choose extracts which show you coping well with a difficult customer or securing a sale. Stills can include examples of good quality work that you have completed, especially if it is visually appealing. Photographs can also be fitted into the template, but they need to have their own intrinsic appeal from, for example, the location they're taken in or their context.

Before you can put together any kind of portfolio compilation, you need to work on the basic materials that you will want to include. That is the purpose of this exercise, i.e. to log the types of material you would use and to work out how you would put them together. If you can go one step further and actually start compiling the information, then that will be all to the good. But this isn't essential at this point.

Whether or not you actually collate any source material, you will still need to write your overarching narrative with its pointers to information subsets. The style needs to be punchy, but it should also include recruitment-friendly buzzwords. These tend to change with alarming rapidity, so be aware of the appropriate terminology to use. The best place to find the buzzwords of the moment is in recruitment advertisements in specialized journals which cover your sector of expertise, although articles in personnel and recruitment journals provide clues as well.

Let's work on the design of your digital portfolio now, and come back to some practicalities once you have explored the disciplines of putting a portfolio together for yourself.

Designing your digital portfolio

Step 1 – The Architecture

Begin by working out the headings that you want to use for your achievements, skills, attitudes and all the other talents that make you employable. Think also about the keywords you're going to use.

There's a balance to be achieved here. Words like "qualifications", "address" and "current position" won't do for a search engine what digging up buried treasure in the garden might do for a human being's pulse rate. But if you're too sophisticated, with labels like "intellectual assets", "cyberpod" and "current manpower cell", you could get missed – or rejected – too.

Now list your keyword headings.

YOUR DIGITAL PORTFOLIO ARCHITECTURE
Keyword headings for each portfolio section
-
-
-
-
-
-
-
-

Step 2 – Logging the available material

For the next stage, draw up a list of all the material you might be able to include in your portfolio. This is your longlist of items which might or might not go into your portfolio, depending on the circumstances. You will need a selection of material to choose from, as different employers will stress different criteria in relation to the people they want for a particular contract.

First list in the left-hand column the keyword headings you came up with in step 1. Then alongside the most appropriate heading, log the material you already have, e.g. your qualifications, or evidence you could easily get hold of having already negotiated permissions, e.g. specimens of your work (if appropriate), or evidence of your employer recognizing the quality of your work.

For each item you list in the middle column, log in the right-hand column the medium or media that the material consists of, e.g. text, sound, combination of sound and moving image, etc.

MATERIAL AVAILABLE FOR YOUR DIGITAL PORTFOLIO

Keyword headings	Existing material	Media
1	•	•
	•	•
	•	•
2	•	•
	•	•
	•	•
3	•	•
	•	•
	•	•

4	•	•
	•	•
	•	•
5	•	•
	•	•
	•	•
6	•	•
	•	•
	•	•
7	•	•
	•	•
	•	•
8	•	•
	•	•
	•	•

Step 3 – Identifying material to fill the gaps

Now work out what's missing from your portfolio under which categories. Where does it look light or unconvincing? Work on how you can contrive experiences that will enable you to fill in the gaps.

There will be areas which you will conclude are strong or certainly adequate, so you won't need to do this part of the activity for all the headings which you have identified. You will be able to leave some of the sections blank, then.

For the headings which you do complete, you will again need to itemize the evidence, indicate the media in which you would want the evidence to be presented, and then in the right-hand (fourth) column, write down how you intend to obtain the evidence, e.g. negotiation with your employer, witness statement by a third party, and so on. This "access plan" will require some thought, so don't expect to be able to complete this part of the activity in a single session.

Start by listing the relevant headings in the left column. These are from your digital portfolio architecture keyword headings which you have already completed in step 1. Then list in the second column, the items of evidence you would use to back each of the keyword headings. Then for each item of evidence state in the third column the medium or media it would be shown in. And finally, in the fourth column, write down how you intend to get the evidence, i.e. your access plan.

GENERATING NEW MATERIAL FOR YOUR DIGITAL PORTFOLIO

Keyword headings	New material	Media	Access plan
1	•	•	•
	•	•	•
	•	•	•
2	•	•	•
	•	•	•
	•	•	•
3	•	•	•
	•	•	•
	•	•	•
4	•	•	•
	•	•	•
	•	•	•
5	•	•	•
	•	•	•
	•	•	•
6	•	•	•
	•	•	•
	•	•	•
7	•	•	•
	•	•	•
	•	•	•
8	•	•	•
	•	•	•

Step 4 – Completing the narrative

Finally, you need to write your narrative text, which knits the whole portfolio together. Look again at the case study example of Mark Richards given earlier in this chapter, to get an idea of the kind of style and flow of expression that might be appropriate.

Don't wait until you have acquired all the material you have logged in step 3 before completing this part of the activity. You will be revising it constantly in any event. Above all, it's important that you have some text that can encapsulate your value to an employer as early as possible in your planning for the global market. If it's done properly, it will increase your motivation as well as keep you constantly on the look-out for attractive and convincing portfolio material.

OVERARCHING NARRATIVE FOR YOUR DIGITAL PORTFOLIO

(The overall structure, shape and content of your portfolio narrative is for you to determine. You might want to look again at the specimen extract from Mark Richards' digital portfolio reproduced earlier in this chapter.)

Portfolio disciplines

You should seek to negotiate with your employer, or any other provider of sources for your portfolio, permission to use the material. You will need to exercise caution here. If you're not confident that your employer will be supportive, then just complete the whole activity privately, as a planning exercise. We have seen that some employers still have old-fashioned values which classify any hint of eventually wanting to work elsewhere as industrial treachery.

Make a habit of updating the material you have gathered. Throw out the sources that show you involved in work that's dated, or as you gain new evidence that demonstrates each particular strength or skill more convincingly than the material you already have. Monthly updating not only saves you having to do a lot of work when the time comes, but it reinforces the mindset of engineering situations that will show you as an attractive prospect to a potential employer or contract manager.

Even if you're not able to put together all aspects of what you would want to have included on your digital portfolio, there's no need to feel concerned. The aim of this activity is to make you aware, in all that you do, which elements of your work would be most effective if presented as part of a self-marketing exercise.

As you log your potential evidence bites, you will see yourself increasingly as others would see you, and your work performance will acclimatize to the changing needs of employers and contract managers as a result. In addition, as the technology becomes ubiquitous, you will be ahead of the game in sifting the high-class material from the rest, and thereby developing an eye (and an ear) for the most effective types of material to incorporate into your digital portfolio.

Thinking for the global market

Creating your own digital portfolio requires more than the ability to compile a summary of your career so far from the raw material that just happens to be available. It needs:

- the willingness to diagnose your strengths and weaknesses for the market segment you're working in or have ambitions to operate in
- the imagination to exploit all the advantages of IT in order to market yourself effectively
- the negotiating skills to forge continuously opportunities to demonstrate and record your abilities for inclusion in your portfolio materials bank
- sufficient knowledge of the recruitment market to enable you to design your portfolio and place it to ensure optimum exploitation of the available networks
- commitment to constant career planning, monitoring and review of your progress.

Conclusion: And Beyond the Portfolio ...?

I began this book with an affirmation of the future. Security is achievable even after the demise of the job for life.

What about the long-term prospects for the portfolio? Surely it too will succumb to the relentless forces of economic competition and technological advance? Perhaps if we pursue the logic of the polycontractual workers which we explored in chapters 2 and 7, there will come a point at which all the generation, compilation and selection of appropriate multimedia materials will be done for us. Perhaps we can look forward to the grind eventually being taken out of portfolio management with the arrival of the individually customized mother of all search engines.

In the meantime we can maintain our optimism about the future of our employability. There are more jobs and a higher proportion of working-age people employed now than at any time in history. There has been a massive incorporation of women into paid work in all industrialized societies.

There is no law of diminishing employment activity. Contract opportunities are created at the same time as they are terminated. Countless opportunities arise constantly from a world where global competition is redefining products, markets, processes and economic inputs, including capital and information.

Neither is there an inexorable decline in the volume of human effort required, as a result of the advance of information technology. The quantitative relationship between employment losses and employment gains depends on a broader range of factors associated with competitiveness, government policy, institutional environments and relative position in the global economy.

Overall, the employment projections of the Organization for Economic Development and Co-operation countries are for moderate growth in jobs in the European Union and Japan up to 2005, with more significant growth in the USA.

To be sure, a secure future, understood as a sufficient income stream to cover the needs of a lifetime, won't be available to everyone. There won't be room for the computer illiterate, for network isolates, or for the majority of those living in the under-communicated territories.

The intensity of risk is increasing. On the surface societies are becoming polarized, with a substantial top and bottom growing at both ends of the occupational structure while the middle is shrinking – all at varying paces depending upon each country's position in the international division of labour and upon its political climate.

So it takes commitment and self-belief to meet the challenge of achieving economic security. But applying your energy to that ambition is itself personally fulfilling as well as potentially rewarding financially.

The core message of this book has been the critical importance of forging as many links to the global economy as you possibly can, through your work base, your communication skills, your networking ability, your commitment to marketing yourself – through a host of opportunities arising from your:

- skills
- knowledge
- expertise
- attitudes
- personality traits
- experience
- contacts
- communication networks
- use of technology.

This amalgam of skills and experiences will together form an asset base from which we will network our contract bids in pursuit of personal security and achievement. It is, after all, the network which has emerged as the pivotal organizational form of the in-formation age: stock exchange markets; financial institutions managing global financial flows; political networks, from Euro-pean parliamentary groupings to shadowy association between international terrorists; the intricacy of organization involved in producing, distributing and laundering the profits from the sale of illicit drugs; complex media networks bringing instant news to our TV screens; the highly developed links created by fringe religious entities such as the Aum Shinrikyo sect in Japan, appealing to a young and highly educated élite, mixing spirituality, advanced technology and millenarian doom.

In his classic sociological analysis, Manuell Castells (1996) has shown how we live in an economy organized around global networks of capital management and information, whose access to technology constitutes the root of productivity and competitiveness.

The process of adding value within a production process organized around information and communication technology, whether it relates to production of goods or delivery of services, requires role differentiation among workforces which can be characterized as:

- leadership: planning and strategic decision making
- research: product and process innovation
- design: adaptation, packaging and targeting of innovation
- integration: relationship management, co-ordinating the effort and reconciling the priorities of those involved in leadership, research, design and execution
- the operational function: execution of tasks under workers' own initiative and with workers applying their own understanding
- the robotic function: the execution of ancillary, pre-programmed tasks which aren't reducible to mechanized or digital automation.

Against this typology we can set another dimension in the networked economy, i.e. the need and capacity for the performer to integrate his or her effort with that of other workers, whether they're all in the same organization or part of a local, regional or global network. This dimension is the relational capacity, with functions differentiated according to three levels:

- the networkers set up the connections on their own initiative, connecting the various stands of the network enterprise
- the networked, i.e. on-line workers who communicate but on the basis of other people's directions
- the unnetworked: workers tied to specific tasks, defined by receipt of instructions, for which no initiative is required.

Finally there is the decision-making continuum:

- the decision makers, who take the final decision

- the participants, who play their part in influencing the decision
- the executors, who carry out the decision.

Although this is a somewhat synthetic representation of the main distinguishing features in the nature of task performance within informational work processes, it's clear how, in each case, the skills for the global market which you have explored (and activated through your own responses to the related activities) throughout this book have focused on the acquisition of the assets which need to be developed for individuals to have the capacity to discharge the higher-order skills identified with respect to each of these dimensions.

Thus the human resource assets needed for successful inter-action with the networks which will increasingly dominate our lives replicate those needed to meet the challenge of maintaining employability in the global market.

If this book has helped you to focus the direction of your ambitions for your long-term employability and potential for personal development and fulfilment, then it will have achieved its purpose. If it has made you think more deeply about the nature of work in the global economy and to reflect upon your experiences in the light of your analysis, can I invite you to share those thoughts and experiences with me by contacting me at the e-mail address given in the preface to this book.

I have no doubt that there's a rich vein of imagination and experience waiting to be analysed and disseminated for the benefit of new generations of aspirants to global security.

References and Further Reading

Barnado's (1996). *Young People's Social Attitudes*.

Barnatt, Christopher (1995). *Cyber Business Mindsets for a Wired Age*.

Bridges, William (1994). *Jobshift*.

British Youth Council (1996). *Never Had it So Good?*

Brown, Phillip, and Lauder, Hugh (1996). Education, globalization and economic development. *Journal of Education Policy*, 11, pp. 1–25.

Castells, Manuel (1996). *The Information Age: Economy, Society and Culture, Vol. 1: The Rise of the Network Society*.

Confederation of British Industry (1995). *Realising the Vision: A Skills Passport*.

Davis, Steven, Haltiwanger, John, and Schuh, Scott (1996). *Job Creation and Destruction*.

Demos (1995). *Generation X and the New Work Ethic*.

Durlacher Multimedia (1996). *The Internet in 1996 – an Investment Perspective*.

Ellison, Robin, Houston, Nicola, and Tinsley, Kevin (1997). British labour force projections: 1997–2006, *Labour Market Trends*, February, pp. 51–59.

Fukuyama, Francis (1995). *Trust: The Social Virtues and the Creation of Prosperity*.

Handy, Charles (1989). *The Age of Unreason*.

Handy, Charles (1994). *The Empty Raincoat: Making Sense of the Future*.

Handy, Charles (1995). *Beyond Certainty: The Changing Worlds of Organisations*.

Industrial Relations Services (1995). *Graduate Recruitment and Sponsorship: The 1995 IRS Survey of Employer Practice*.

Industry in Education (1996). *Towards Employability*.

Institute for Employment Research (1996). *Review of the Economy and Employment: Occupational Studies*.

Institute of Management (1995). *Survey of Long-term Employment Strategies*.

International Monetary Fund (1996). *Have North–South Growth Linkages Changed?*

International Survey Research (1996). *Employee Satisfaction: Tracking European Trends*.

Kennedy, Joyce, and Morrow, Thomas (1995). *Electronic Résumé Revolution*.

Market and Opinion Research International (1996). *Women: Setting New Priorities*.

Marshall, Judi (1996). *Women Managers Moving on: Exploring Career and Life Choices*.

McRae, Hamish (1996). *The World in 2020 – Power, Culture and Prosperity: A Vision of the Future*.

Metcalf, Hilary (ed.) (1995). *Future Skill Demand and Supply: Trends, Shortages and Gluts*.

Moss Kanter, Rosabeth (1996). *World Class: Thriving Locally in the Global Economy*.

New Ways to Work (1996). *Balanced Lives: Changing Work Patterns for Men*.

Pemberton, Carole (1995). *Strike a New Career Deal*.

Peters, Tom (1994). *The Tom Peters Seminar: Crazy Times Call for Crazy Organisations*.

Quah, Danny (1996). *The Invisible Hand and the Weightless Economy*.

Socio-Economic Statistics and Analysis Group of the Office for National Statistics. *Labour Force Survey Quarterly Bulletin*.

Spectrum Strategy Consultants (1996). *Development of the Information Society: An International Analysis*.

Vogl, Frank, and Sinclair, James (1996). *Boom: Visions and Insights for Creating Wealth in the 21st Century*.

Von Zugbach, Reggie (1995). *The Winning Manager*.

Wes, Marina (1996). *Globalisation: Winners and Losers*.

Useful websites

BT Labs
www.labs.bt.com
Institute of Management
www.inst-mgt.org.uk
International Labour Organization
www.ilo.org
Organization for Economic Co-operation and Development
www.oecd.org
Skills and Enterprise Network
www.open.gov.uk/dfee/skilnet/senhome.htm
Socio-Economic Statistics and Analysis Group of the Office for
National Statistics
www.open.gov.uk/lmsd/lfsddata.htm
Yahoo pointers to language resources
www.yahoo.com/Education/Languages/

Index

Abbey National, 35, 62
Abitur, 114
Accountants, 9, 13, 41, 100, 124, 164
Administration, 9, 13, 26, 34, 99
Advertising, 5, 37, 39, 84, 113
Africa, 80, 92, 94–5
Ageism, 116, 206–7
Agriculture, 25
Agrochemicals, 27
Allen, Paul, 101
Allied Domecq, 63, 129–30, 151, 154, 175, 177
Amer, Stefan, 162
Andreessen, Marc, 38
Anglian Water, 12–13, 64, 125, 153–4
Annualized hours, 6, 65
Architects, 5, 36, 102
Arms to Iraq affair, 31
Asia, 80, 92–4, 96, 101, 113, 115–16, 151, 161, 164, 174
Associated Examining Board, 114
Association of Graduate Recruiters, 86, 128
Aum Shinrikyo, 222

Baker, Yvonne, 59
Bangkok, 174
Banking, 11, 25, 37, 164
Barclays, 87
Barnatt, Christopher, 99
Bath University School of Management, 53
BBC, 199
Beal, Derek, 86
Belgium, 167
Biotechnology, 113
Bissell, Christopher, 117–18, 170
Bombay, 174
Bouzy, Louis-Dominique, 149–50, 182

Bratt, Jonathan, 57, 115, 155, 182
Brewster, Chris, 57, 128, 155, 163, 200
Bridges, William, 4
Brighouse, Jacquie, 185–6
British Chambers of Commerce, 170
British Petroleum, 62
British Telecommunications, 11–12, 31, 45, 48, 51, 54, 62, 64, 75, 119–20, 154
British–American Tobacco, 86, 92
Building, 5, 98, 163
Burtons, 127
Business services, 25
Business Strategies, 2, 7

Cable Communications Association, 12
Caine, Terry, 158
Caller line identification, 30, 34
Canada, 59, 147
Career:
  corporate, 54–5, 57–9, 65–7
  global, 90, 98, 100, 102, 139, 141, 150–3, 155, 160, 162, 165–9, 171, 175, 180–1, 187–9, 192, 195, 206
  strategy, 1, 3–5, 8, 13, 18–19, 23, 53, 58, 67, 72–4, 90, 97–8, 102–3, 119, 121, 123–4, 130, 139–40, 155, 167, 194, 205, 219
Careers Europe, 158
Carey, Mick, 158
Castells, Manuel, 222
Catering, 6, 10, 26, 97, 137
Caxton, William, 30
Chemicals, 7, 25, 118
China, 82, 91, 94, 151, 155–7, 161, 166, 174, 178, 183

Chinese, overseas, 82
Civil engineering, 152
Civil service, 7, 163
Clarke, James, 101
Cleaning, 13, 26, 97, 111, 163
Clerical occupations, 2, 26, 99
Cochrane, Peter, 31
Compaq, 7
Competition, 10, 13, 80, 83, 94–6,
    113–14, 122, 155, 160–1, 165,
    194, 199, 220, 222
Composers, 5
Computer telephony integration, 30,
    34–5
Confederation of British Industry, 63,
    114, 119, 127, 129
Consultancy, 2, 41, 43, 59–60, 113,
    171, 196, 205, 210
Coopers & Lybrand, 114
Countries:
  developed, 5, 160
  developing, 10, 80–2, 101
Craft occupations, 26, 103, 137
Cranfield University, 57, 128, 154–5,
    162–3, 200
CV, 4, 28, 36, 76, 86, 88–9, 158–9,
    191–2, 194–5, 198–201, 203–4,
    211

Davis, Steven, 13
Delayering, 12, 26
Deloitte Touche Tohmatsu, 96
Dematerialized economy, 110
Demos, 57
Denmark, 91, 174
Department for Education and
    Employment, 25, 122
Designers, 5, 10, 13, 121
Digital goods, 42
Digital literacy, 42
Distribution, 25, 78, 100
Dixons, 127
DNA sequencing, 45, 111–12
Dow Chemical, 87
Downshifting, 53, 58, 67, 73, 152
Downsizing, 11–12, 44, 58, 64, 180,
    187
Duke of Edinburgh's Award, 90, 121
Durham University, 155, 178
Durlacher Multimedia, 38

EAP, 92
Economy, the dematerialized, 111–12,
    210
Education, 7–8, 10, 16, 24–5, 27, 32,
    42–4, 55, 62, 80–1, 89, 91, 101,
    110–11, 113–21, 124–8, 130–4,
    136–7, 139, 148, 150, 166–7,
    169, 174–5, 188–9, 196–8, 202
Employability, 5, 56, 62, 64, 67, 75,
    119–20, 122, 124, 127–8, 131,
    203, 220, 223
Employers' views, 6–7, 62–4, 67, 114,
    119–24, 127–30, 133, 158, 175,
    179, 198–9, 202–3, 206–7, 215,
    218
Employment:
  female, 1, 3
  male, 1
  part-time, 2–3, 6–8
  temporary, 2–3, 6–8
Engineering, 7, 12, 25, 122, 126,
    137, 149, 158, 164
Erskine, 7
Euro qualification programme, 163
Europe, 1–3, 82, 91–3, 95–6, 158,
    162–3
Eastern, 94, 180
Europe Car Interrent, 167
European Commission, 6, 160, 162,
    172–3
European Information Service, 122
European Union, 2–3, 6, 11, 37, 41,
    82, 84, 91, 94, 96, 122, 145,
    150, 158, 161–3, 165, 167, 173,
    221
European Voluntary Service for
    Young People, 162
European, The, 162, 198–9
Expatriates, 148–50, 152

Federation of Small Businesses, 37
Financial services, 6, 13, 35, 37–8,
    40, 99, 111, 113, 126, 161, 221
Flexible contracts, 6–9, 65, 197
Food and drink sector, 25
Forbes World League Table, 101
Ford, 62, 83, 87
Fordism, 113
France, 114, 158
Frankfurt, 99, 145

Fujitsu, 33
Fukuyama, Francis, 116
Future of work debate, 1, 3–4, 9, 63, 194, 220

Gates, Bill, 101
General National Vocational Qualifications, 124
Germany, 3, 95, 102, 114, 158, 163, 170–1
Gershuny, Jonathan, 52
GHN, 121
Global communication skills, 3, 41, 91, 168, 171, 188, 190–1, 221
Global economy, 1, 40, 61, 79–80, 84, 94–5, 108, 110, 113, 117, 124, 166, 173–4, 192, 220–1,223
Global nomad, 141–193
Global professional associations, 102–3, 166
Globalization, 26, 41, 80–1, 86–7, 101, 112, 160, 165–6
Graduates, 8, 26–7, 56–7, 86, 92, 117, 119, 127–9, 154, 158, 162, 196
Great Depression, 1, 94
GTM Entrepose, 149
Guatemala, 147

Haltiwanger, John, 13
Handy, Charles, 4–5, 97–8, 208
Hawkins, Debra, 59–61
Health services, 3, 9–10, 25, 36, 43, 79, 102, 111, 137, 150, 210
Healy, Michelle, 86
Higher education, 114, 119–21, 124, 129, 136, 162, 167, 186–7
Highfliers Research, 162
Homeworking, 40, 66, 94–5
Hong Kong, 82, 92, 161, 174
Hotels sector, 10, 25

IBM, 8, 83
ICL, 38
India, 82, 92, 94–6, 166
Industrial Relations Services, 120
Industrial Revolution, 9, 78, 143
Industry in Education, 8, 125, 127–8, 131, 171

Information and communication technology, 9, 11–12, 29, 41–2, 79–80 111, 117, 125, 142, 180, 222
Information technology sector, 164, 196–7
Information/knowledge society, 9, 11–12, 26, 30–2, 42, 78–9, 81–2, 84, 95, 97–101, 110, 112–13, 115–17, 135, 143, 221
INSEAD business school, 59, 88, 151, 170, 182
Institute for Employment Research, 9, 25–6
Institute of Management, 3, 6
Insurance sector, 11, 25
Intel, 111
International Hedgehog Registry, 37
International Labour Organization, 94
Internet, the, 30, 37–40, 45, 79, 101, 142, 168, 198, 204
Interpreters, 41–2, 168, 171–3
Intranets, 30, 39–40
Investors in People, 62, 122
Irish Republic, 11, 162

J. C. Keepsake Diamond, 37
Jackson, Bridget, 145–6, 151, 183–4
Jakarta, 174
James, Stephanie, 170
Japan, 91, 96, 102, 113–14, 116, 177, 221–2
Jennings, Mike, 56
Job interviews, 86–7, 120, 134, 138–9, 158, 200, 202, 207

Kalinowski, Michal, 56
Kennedy, Joyce, 200
Kingsley, Jane, 76, 155, 166
KITE, 96
Knight, Ruth, 185–6
Knowledge sector, 12, 189
Kuala Lumpur, 174

Labour:
    skilled, 7, 10–11, 26, 41, 95, 114, 166
    unskilled, 7, 10, 26
Labour force projections (UK), 1

Labour market, 1–2, 4, 20, 24–5, 27, 56–7, 62, 64, 77, 125, 127–30, 174
  global, 1–2, 4, 40–1, 77, 79, 81, 97–8, 102, 109, 126, 144, 158, 162–3, 167, 170, 175, 198–9, 207
Languages, 35, 41–2, 91–3, 109, 114, 121, 128, 136, 158, 166–76, 179, 189–90, 192–3
Leisure sector, 3
Life-work balance, 53, 55, 67, 70
Lifetime/lifelong learning, 130–1
Lincoln, Denise, 63, 129–30, 151, 154–5, 175–7, 181, 187
Lithuania, 185
Local Enterprise Companies, 25
Local government, 8, 64
Logica, 87–8
Logistics, 43
London, 99, 161
Luddites, 9
Lufthansa, 154
Luxembourg, 174

MacTemps, 199
Managers, 3, 11–13, 26, 54, 57, 92, 97, 153, 163, 166, 171
Manila, 161
Manton, Monique, 185–6
Manufacturing, 1, 7, 9–10, 12, 26, 81, 94, 98, 111, 165, 197
Marakon Associates, 177
Marketing sector, 34, 41, 113
Marks and Spencer, 92
Marshall, Judi, 53–4
Mass production, 83, 113, 125, 197
Massidda, Diego, 152
McMahon, Rory, 172–4, 178, 180, 182–3
McNally, Eryl, MEP, 114, 118–19, 166, 171
McRae, Hamish, 83–4
Media, the, 113, 221
Melbourne, 161
Mercedes Benz, 83
Metals, 7, 25
Metcalf, Hilary, 122
Mexico, 177
Microelectronics, 113

Microsoft, 101
Midland Bank, 127
Milmore, Mark, 38
Minerals, 7, 25
Mintel, 161
Mobility, 3, 73, 85, 144, 153, 162–3, 167, 188–91
Moore's Law, 111
Moore, Gordon, 111
Morgan, Philip, 54–5, 58
Morrow, Thomas, 200
Moscow, 185–6
Moss Kanter, Rosabeth, 40, 83, 99
Multicultural teams, 56, 93, 151, 153, 179–80, 190, 193, 209
Multimedia, 32, 36, 38–9, 42, 44, 201, 203, 211, 220
Multinational companies, 40, 65, 80, 83, 86, 89, 91–2, 100, 114–15, 150, 155, 160, 164, 171
Musicians, 5, 137

National Institute for Economic and Social Research, 95
National Vocational Qualifications, 118
Netherlands, the, 91, 158, 171, 174
Netscape, 38, 101
Networking, 32, 43–4, 58, 73, 77, 80, 85, 93, 99–100, 102, 109, 128, 144, 160–1, 166, 192, 196, 201, 221–3
New York, 99, 161, 163
Nielsen, A.C., 57, 115, 155, 182
Norway, 174
Norwich Union, 62

Okorocha, Eunice, 181
Open University, 117, 170
Operation Raleigh, 121
Optical fibre technology, 78, 97
Organization for Economic Co-operation and Development, 10, 94, 127–8, 165
Outsourcing, 13, 81
Overseas Placing Unit, 158
Ovum, 34

Paisley University, 57

Peachey, Mike, 148–9
Pemberton, Carole, 63
Perkins, Stephen, 57
Personnel services, 13, 41
Personnel Today, 6,
Peterborough Software, 6
Peters, Tom, 7
Plantime, 6
Policy Studies Institute, 122
Polycontractual workers, 35–6, 201,
    220
Portfolio
    career, 5, 8, 29, 57, 76, 88, 90, 98,
        109, 191, 220
    digital, 194–219
Portfolio workers, 4–5, 35, 42, 65–7,
    98, 126, 208–9
Portugal, 88–9, 163
PowerGen, 148
Price Waterhouse, 56
Procter and Gamble, 92
Psychological contract, 8, 52–3,
    65, 67
Public sector, 6–8, 111, 138–9
Pundsnes, Per, 145, 169, 184

Quah, Danny, 112
Qualifications, 27, 89–90, 110,
    113–16, 118–19, 124–5, 127,
    143, 148, 158, 163–4, 194, 196,
    199–201, 206–7, 211

Rank Xerox, 176
Red Spider, 99
Redundancy, 7–8, 11, 35, 53–4, 56–8,
    67
Reed Personnel Services, 86
Retail sector, 10–11
Reuters, 87
Richards, Mark, 211–12
Rink, Alex, 58–9, 88–9, 146–7, 170,
    183
Robertson, Charlie, 99
Royal Automobile Club, 34
Russell Reynolds Associates, 76, 155,
    166
Russia, 171, 174, 182, 185–6

Samaritans, the, 39
San Francisco, 161

Satellite technology, 96–97
SCB Warburg, 86
Schuh, Scott, 13
Science, 26, 50, 114
Scott Report, 31
Secretarial work, 26, 31, 97
Self-employment, 2, 7–8, 73
Self-investment/development, 4, 44,
    51, 63–4, 67, 93, 97, 119, 133,
    138, 195–6
Service sector, 2, 6, 10, 12, 26, 35,
    42, 111, 113, 165
Shalit, Jonathan, 155
Shanghai Conservatory of Music,
    157
Shell, 92
Sigmund Shalit & Associates, 155
Sinclair, James, 80
Singapore, 92, 114, 166, 174
Single European currency, 95,
    165
Skills and Enterprise Network,
    25
Smith, Kitson, 92
Social services, 3, 111
Social workers, 7
Socrates programme, 162
Sony, 33
South Africa, 94
South America, 80, 96
St Petersburg, 185
Standard Chartered, 91
Steele, Richard, 59, 177
Stewart Scott, 152
Stock, Jonathan, 155–7 169, 178–9,
    183
Strategic Remuneration Research
    Centre, 57
Surrey University, 181
Sweden, 102, 162
Swedish National Union of Students,
    162
SwissAir, 96
Switzerland, 91, 96, 167, 171
Sydney, 161
Systran, 172

Taylor, David, 64, 120, 122, 125,
    153–4
Taylorism, 117

Teamwork, 11, 40, 56, 62, 87, 93, 113, 115–17, 119–21, 128–30, 151, 166–7, 175–6, 190, 199, 202, 205, 209
Technology, 4, 7, 10–12, 26, 29–51, 66, 79–80, 82–3, 93, 96, 100, 102, 109, 111, 113–14, 117, 122, 125, 127, 131, 142, 149, 154, 164, 180, 192, 196–7, 199–201, 206–7, 209–10, 218, 220–2
Telecommunications, 6, 11–12, 29–31, 35, 41, 79, 95–7, 99, 113, 196
Telesales, 34
Teleworking, 6, 40
Textiles, 25
Thailand, 151
Times Newspapers, 168
Tobin, Colm, 56, 162
Tokyo, 99, 174
Toronto, 161
Training, 9, 27, 51, 56–8, 62, 89, 110, 113–14, 116, 118, 121, 123–6, 128, 138, 154, 163, 175, 196–8, 201
Training and Enterprise Councils, 25
Translation software, 30, 42, 172
Translators, 41, 158, 168, 171–3
Transport, 25, 96
Turnbull, George, 114
Tyson, Rachel, 60–1, 181

United Nations, 101
University College Dublin, 56, 162
Universum International, 56

USA, 91–2, 95–6, 101–2, 111–12, 114, 221
Utilities, 25

Vancouver, 161
Vauxhall, 62, 127
Videocommunication, 33, 79, 86, 199
Videoconferencing, 32–3, 39, 51, 86, 190, 200, 213
Vietnam, 151, 187
Virtual companies, 40, 43, 99, 100
Virtual Language Library, 179
Virtual reality, 30, 36
Vogl, Frank, 80
Von Zugbach, Reggie, 57–8

Warwick University, 9
Webb, Tony, 63–4, 119, 129
Welford, Susan, 185–6
Whitcutt, Dick, 8, 124–5, 127–9, 171
Whitehead Selection, 86
Whitehead, Graham, 54, 64, 75–6, 119–20, 181
Wholesale sector, 11
Wilson, Abbi, 59
Wong, Susanna, 152, 178, 182–3
Work experience, 123, 167, 204
World Economic Forum, 114
World Wide Web, 38–9, 179, 211

Youth for Europe, 162

Zurich, 99